BLASTED BY ADVERSITY

BLASTED BY ADVERSITY

The Making of a Wounded Warrior

BY LUKE MURPHY WITH JULIE BETTINGER

INKSHARES

Written by Luke Murphy with Julie Bettinger
Edited by Girl Friday Productions
Design by MacFadden & Thorpe

Published by Inkshares, Inc. in Oakland, California
Printed in the United States of America
Second Edition

2 3 4 5 6 7 8 9 10 1

Library of Congress Control Number: 2015933768
ISBN 978-1-947848-81-8

This book is dedicated to my fiancéee, family, friends, those I served with, and all the men and women who have ever donned a uniform to defend our country. It's also dedicated to all those affected by our service and our injuries.

AUTHOR'S NOTE

Everyone remembers life events differently, and everyone has their own opinion. This story is told the way I remember it and from my personal point of view. Not everyone involved could be mentioned, specifically, and some names have been changed. You know who you are.

TABLE OF CONTENTS

PROLOGUE

Chapter 1: Blown Up   5

Chapter 2: My Life Is about to Change   11

Chapter 3: Holy Terror   17

Chapter 4: My Heisman Moment   24

Chapter 5: The Enemy from Within   30

Chapter 6: Mission to the Future   36

Chapter 7: It's War, and I'm Going Regular Army   42

Chapter 8: Choosing the Rakkasans   47

Chapter 9: At the Ready   58

Chapter 10: Her Fantasy, My Nightmare   66

Chapter 11: Tip of the Spear   70

Chapter 12: Hanging from the Hood of a Humvee   77

Chapter 13: Like a Good Marine   87

Chapter 14: Stop-Loss   94

Chapter 15: Differences   103

Chapter 16: Blue Door Alley   114

Chapter 17: Premonitions   125

Chapter 18: What We Remember   131

Chapter 19: Blast-Wound Guys   140

Chapter 20: The Nurse in Charge   148

Chapter 21: Comeback   170

Chapter 22: Slopes and Amputees   176

Chapter 23: Ice Hockey and Paybacks   185

Chapter 24: Meeting Mary   190

Chapter 25: Man of Steele   196

Chapter 26: Let Me Speak   204

Chapter 27: Finding a Future   211

Chapter 28: Hammertoes   220

Chapter 29: Fish Story   225

Chapter 30: More Than a Project   233

Chapter 31: What Lasts   243

EPILOGUE   250

Acknowledgments

About the Authors

Photo Credits

Backers Page

PROLOGUE

It was a blazing July afternoon in 2006, but the rehab floor at the Walter Reed Army Medical Center near Washington, DC, was icebox cold. My hour of physical therapy was done and I had moved on to occupational. The arm amputees were working one-on-one with therapists across a desk, while I stayed with the hand weights to strengthen my wrists and grip, working from my wheelchair. It had been four months since the blast, and after twenty-six surgeries I was down to a scrawny 124 pounds, from my "fighting weight" of 193.

The atmosphere was a lot like a football locker room, except for the missing limbs. If you focused only on our faces, you'd see the determined look of athletes. You'd hear the grunting and forced exhales during exercises and pointed jabs between Army soldiers and Marines as we ragged on each other. It was like being with my guys again—my Joes—and I felt good.

Across the room, I saw a knot of uniforms and business suits. VIPs were flocking around a dark-haired woman who looked vaguely familiar, another celebrity tour, I guessed, visiting the amputee petting zoo. She scanned the room, as people around her tried to direct her attention. I kept moving, focusing intently on my workout, when I sensed her entourage closing in on me. Someone said, "Hey, soldier, Cher wants to say hello."

I didn't look up right away. I figured I'd give her a chance to take it all in. Here I was, a twenty-four-year-old with a bare stump covered in surgical staples where my right leg used to be, and wearing a giant metal cage on my left leg. I had two pins going straight through my left knee, another six from there to my ankle, and two more anchoring the foot. Every time I strained my upper body, my lower body leaked blood, so my left sock was stained reddish brown. Still, maybe I looked more inviting than the guys dragging IV poles, with tangles of tubes coming out of their veins, or the ones who were still discolored from iodine baths—new amputees, who had just arrived from Afghanistan and Iraq.

I looked at Cher sideways over the hand weight, and she met my eyes. "So, what's your story?" she asked.

I could hear my dad's repeated warnings from all the visits playing in my head: "Please don't say anything embarrassing. For once, Luke, can't you just be nice?" But before I knew it, the sarcastic me answered: "Oh, I was just playing with matches."

So what *is* my story? I like to think I'm just a regular guy. A young kid from a small town in South Florida who watched Westerns and war movies and had a burning desire to be a soldier. A guy who convinced his dad to sign a contract that allowed me to enter the Florida National Guard as a junior in high school. And someone who, after 9/11, put college on hold to protect Miami International Airport in my first active-duty assignment.

At that time, I also had a curiosity that couldn't be tamed. Veterans told me how wild and scary war could be, but I had to see for myself. I wanted to answer that calling I'd had since I was a little kid: to serve my country like my dad, my friend's dad, and my grandfather. Growing up, my family called me "Lucky Luke," and I guess you could say I added to that nickname by becoming a member of one of the most storied divisions in the US Army—the 101st Airborne—and, within the 101st, getting assigned to the most decorated regiment: the Rakkasans.

Since the injury—the blast—people see my fake leg and say they can't imagine what it's like. And they start asking questions. Many times, these are the same people who can't watch an R movie, but when they see a mangled car on the side of the road, they have to look. They want to know the story. So I tell them, but I'm not doing it for me. I'm telling them for the soldier who can't, the one whose injury goes beyond the physical. The one who feels awkward when someone stops him on the street to say, "Thank you for your service."

That's the main reason I wrote this book: to help give a voice to this new generation of wounded service members.

I've been telling pieces of my story as I travel around the country as a National Campaign Team (NCT) member for the Wounded Warrior Project. NCT members share their stories to raise awareness for the most recently injured servicemen and women while serving as an example of the successes one can achieve after injury. It's therapeutic, a cultural shift from the generations before us, and I don't mind talking candidly about my experiences. With this book, people can hear more of the story. There needs to be a face on the costs of that great American dream people are living. They need to know the human side of it, like the agonizing doubt and extreme loneliness I felt at night in a German hospital when I wondered, *Why didn't I just give it up?* They need to hear about the pain of rehabilitation that a soldier goes through just to relearn the skills of daily living with what has become their "new normal." I want you to meet the self-sacrificing medical personnel who helped put me back together again. I'll introduce you to the crazy guy who came to the Army hospital and told the soldiers—some of whom were missing three limbs—that he wanted to take us skiing in Snowmass, Colorado. You'll also meet the woman named Mary who saw me at one of my lowest moments in the hospital room and proposed I do a marathon. And you'll hear how I answered that challenge about a year after my injury, eventually taking second place in a race in Costa Rica.

There's another reason I wrote this book. I want people to know that while the injury deformed me and caused me unimaginable pain, it will never define me. I have no regrets. I'm thirty-three years old, and I've experienced more than a person could dream of experiencing in three lifetimes. I caught my first yellowfin tuna on Jimmy Buffett's boat. I've climbed mountains in Utah and skied black diamonds, all after the injury. I've spoken to thousands of people at park gatherings and at the Pentagon. I helped start philanthropic organizations that allow service members to enjoy outdoor activities like hunting and fishing. I went back to college at age twenty-seven, pledged a fraternity, and graduated with a degree in less than three years.

Maybe hearing my story will inspire a person to get through whatever is challenging them at the moment. Maybe they'll tell themselves, *If he can do it, I can do it.*

We have a motto in the Rakkasans, etched in our unit insignia: *Ne desit virtus.* Let valor not fail. It takes determination and boldness to face the kinds of dangers that service members face in battle. Some would even say heroic courage or bravery, especially in infantry. To me, it's about attitude. That's the only thing you have control over. And with the right attitude in life, you will not fail.

CHAPTER 1
Blown Up

I wasn't supposed to be there.

My initial tour of duty with the US Army's 187th Infantry Regiment was in 2003. I led a fire team during the invasion of Iraq, which contributed to the 101st Airborne Division's success in liberating three key cities and establishing a free and democratic Iraq. I earned several awards and commendations for exemplary service during Operation Iraqi Freedom, but I came back to the States without some of my buddies. That's war.

By the fall of 2005, my time was up. I had completed nearly six years of service, including a year in Iraq, so the last thing I expected was to be redeployed with twenty-eight days left on my contract. There was a troop shortage, though, so the Army instituted their stop-loss policy. They sent me back to Iraq on a mission leading up to the pre-surge of 2006. At twenty-four years old, I was still one of the youngest squad leaders in the Third Brigade Rakkasans, a unit of roughly four thousand soldiers.

By one o'clock in the morning on Tuesday, April 25, 2006, our twelve-man reconnaissance team had been working twenty-three hours straight without sleep; there were no set shifts with this job. Earlier in the day, we had been on a joint mission in the slums of Sadr City, Baghdad, guarding FBI and CIA agents while they tried to identify mass graves as evidence against Saddam Hussein. We were part of a company of a hundred, but we were grossly outnumbered. The population of the city was about two million with about forty thousand men in the opposition, mostly the Mahdi militia. It was exhausting work.

Patrolling the city might not sound that dangerous to most people, but it can actually be the deadliest kind of work. In the urban areas, you don't know your enemy; you're always getting shot at and dodging bricks thrown by kids. Three years earlier, a little seven-year-old girl walked up and handed a soldier to my left something while we were on foot patrol in Baghdad. It turned out to be an explosive. Four men were injured by the blast, and Sergeant Troy Jenkins from Alabama later died of his injuries.

After the joint mission in Sadr City, we managed to make it back to the base and were trying to wind down when we got the bad news: *You've got to go back into the city.* The brass wanted us to escort a vehicle that had to be out that night, an unusual mission for the Rakkasans.

We made it through the city and headed back to the forward operating base, driving in a convoy. I was the truck commander—the front right passenger—in the second Humvee, and my gunner Adam Jefferson was in the turret behind a .50-caliber machine gun. Neither of us saw the infrared laser. It was attached to the deadliest form of roadside bomb—an explosively formed penetrating (EFP) improvised explosive device (IED), known for its power to pierce almost any type of armored vehicle. It detonated on my side, immediately engulfing us in flames. The blast threw Jefferson's head into the side of the turret, knocking him out temporarily in spite of his helmet; it also mutilated his leg. I felt a huge fireball at the back of my neck. I gulped for air, but toxic fumes burned my esophagus; I had to stop breathing or die.

Heat from the fire ignited chains of ammo that fed into the machine gun from inside the Humvee, causing random explosions.

Boom…boom…boom. With nine grenades in the vehicle, it was only a matter of time before an even bigger explosion.

My M4 rifle, similar to an AR-15, was blown in half. I looked down and lifted my right leg, but my boot stayed on the ground; shrapnel had ripped my leg off at the knee. My left leg was up near my face, blown in half at the calf but still attached by skin. Not good.

The vehicle was still moving, so I ordered the driver to crash into a wall. When we stopped, I pushed on the door with my shoulder. It was caved in from the blast and was now blocked by a ten-foot brick wall. I kept slamming my shoulder into it, until I made enough space to crawl out.

The driver came around to my side and started beating back the flames, thinking I was still inside. I could see him dodging rounds from the machine gun as the heat set off explosions. *Boom…boom…boom.* I tried to yell to him, but nothing came out; my throat was singed. Finally, he looked over and saw me charred and black, lying in a pool of blood, helmet off and clutching my destroyed weapon. I was surrounded by large chunks of the wall that marked the boundary of Sadr City.

I could hear the yelling, the orders, the mass chaos. This time, I wasn't part of it. I could feel myself going to sleep. I knew I was on the way out; I was dying. I started drifting into what felt like an unbelievably great sleep, until I saw an image of my mom. She was wearing a black veil. It looked antique, like the ones I'd seen at my grandma's funeral. She was crying uncontrollably and holding my girlfriend, Kristine. I remember thinking, *I can't do this to my mom.*

Those who have been to war can tell you that oftentimes the last thing a dying soldier will do is scream out for his mom. I guess you get in that vulnerable spot, like you're a kid again. For me, it was a little different. I just remember thinking, *Don't die and do this to your mom.*

So I fought to stay awake, to stay conscious. The medic offered morphine, but I knew he had only one or two doses. I wasn't sure how badly the other guys were hurt so I turned it down. I also knew it would lower my heart rate, and I needed all the adrenaline I could get to stay conscious. As they loaded me onto a stretcher, I heard someone making a medevac request to meet us at the forward operating base.

Our vehicles aren't built for transporting patients, so they balanced me on the backs of two soldiers in the backseat. Someone was trying to shut the Humvee door, but my head was partially blocking it. They didn't realize it and kept slamming harder and harder, slicing into my skull. Nobody could hear my protests. After the third blow, Team Leader John Winton looked back from the front seat to see what was holding us up. He saw the door closing again on my head, screamed, "Stop! Stop!" and then got out and adjusted the stretcher. We went storming off.

Winton kept saying, "Talk to me, Luke."

I groaned, "I don't want to talk, man. It hurts to talk." Nobody understood my esophagus was burned.

He said, "Then just squeeze my hand once in a while." So I kept my eyes shut tight, trying to hold all the pain in one corner of my brain, and squeezed his hand.

Our drivers sped so fast on the dark city roads that we made it to the base in eighteen minutes. I could hear my guys screaming at the guards on the gate to get out of the way: "We got wounded! We got wounded!"

The medevac bird was landing as we pulled in, but they took our gunner, Jefferson, Sergeant Erik Roberts, and me, the only injured, to a tent to be stabilized first. They wanted to make sure we'd survive the flight. When the vehicle stopped, the pain from all the jostling was almost unbearable, maybe an eight on a scale of ten for me. As soon as they started to move me out of the vehicle, it shot to a twelve.

I knew all the medics coming into the tent to meet us; they had worked with us in the past. Now the one who'd gotten a Bronze Star for helping my buddy who was blown up by the little girl was working on me.

I was angry. Our company had dodged some major rounds, and finally our luck was out. But it was never supposed to be me.

I could hear Erik Roberts—like Winton, one of the fast-tracking sergeants in our company. He had been in the back left seat, and the round hit him in the thigh. Roberts was praying, one prayer after another. Our Father, Hail Mary, Glory Be. He was just cycling through prayers as they started the IVs, opened up avenues for blood, and cut off our clothes.

Ten minutes later, they started moving our stretchers to the bird. The soldiers carrying us moved with a purpose across the field, and my pain skyrocketed again. My mind automatically went to managing the action. I knew they would need to put the least wounded on the chopper first, and the guy with the worst injury would go on last, so he could come out first. They put me on last.

Over the roar of the helicopter, I could hear Jefferson moaning. I finally turned to him. "Jefferson!"

"Yeah, Sergeant?"

"What's wrong?"

"It hurts, Sergeant."

I growled, "Quit being a little bitch."

Roberts started laughing and so did Jefferson.

First Sergeant Coroy was outside of the bird and heard us. "The whole company is out here crying, and you guys are in here smokin' and jokin'?" He put my wallet under my head, and the bird took off on its way to Baghdad ER.

When we landed, I remember thinking, *So this is where our soldiers were sent when they got blown up.* They put my stretcher on the back of a John Deere Gator, for a short, bumpy ride to some tents. *Tents?* I thought. I wanted concrete walls. *If I don't have a weapon and I'm not in charge, at least give me a wall.*

I looked around and saw severely wounded everywhere, typical of triage. Baghdad ER is the most state-of-the-art you can get in theater and serves all branches of the military. The next step up is Landstuhl Regional Medical Center in Germany, but they've got to stabilize you to make that four-hour flight. The medics kept me conscious for the next twenty-four hours while they pumped my body full of blood. It was pure agony. Finally, they prepped me for the flight via military aircraft to Landstuhl, and the medic said he was going to put me to sleep.

I woke up on a ventilator in the Landstuhl ICU. And that's where I got my second chance at life.

CHAPTER 2
My Life Is about to Change

A little before nine in the morning on September 11, 2001, I was walking across the parking lot of what is now Indian River State College in Stuart, Florida. It was a bit cloudy, but still summer-like, with temperatures in the high seventies, and there was a decent breeze flowing through the queen palms. I was usually pretty relaxed heading into my speech class, as it never felt like work to me, unlike the rest of my subjects. The assignment the teacher had planned was a prepared improv. Since I was the only college student with military experience, I was supposed to play the soldier. Another student was expected to pose as a flight attendant; there would also be a cop and a news reporter. We were going to be simulating an airplane hijacking, and it was my job to take out the terrorist.

When I walked into the classroom, there was more confusion than usual, and I figured my fellow students had pre-presentation nerves. The teacher held a TV remote in her hand, and the twenty or so students had dropped their books and moved closer to the video monitor. I walked up behind them in time to see an image of the World Trade Center on fire. It was unreal, like a bad joke. Seconds later, we saw another plane crash into the south tower, and I knew something was wrong. Something was majorly wrong.

No one said anything, we just stared at the screen, until finally the teacher turned off the TV and said, "I don't think it's appropriate for us to do our presentation today. Class is cancelled."

As I walked slowly back to my truck, I wondered what was going to happen to me. I mean, I was in the Reserves—and they get called up at times of war. Whatever had just taken place in New York City and, I later learned, the Pentagon was going to affect me personally.

I went straight home, walked into my dad's kitchen, and saw a note on the counter: *Call Army.* I remember thinking, *Here it comes. Do I need to go pack my bags?* I finally reached my dad a few hours later, and he said, no, that note said to call *Amy*, who was a good friend of mine. But my mind was already getting ready.

* * *

It was everything I had been training for, yet not what I expected.

When I'd joined the National Guard in 1999, the US had not been in a significant military action for eight years, since Operation Desert Storm. So the chance of me being in a war seemed unlikely. The thought had crossed my mind, but I'm not the type to dwell on the unknowns. When I enlisted, I was only seventeen years old and mostly looking for a way to build my resume and maybe pay for college. It was my junior year in high school; everyone was talking about plans for the next step after graduation. My older brother had gotten an athletic scholarship for football and wrestling. I played sports, but not at the level that would get anyone's attention. Some military recruiters started visiting our high school, and I always had a little more respect for those who fight for our country. I remember thinking that maybe one day people could look at me the way I always looked at those who served in the military.

My dad was a Marine, and a close friend's dad was a Marine. They didn't talk about their service; they didn't have that secret high five. It was all unspoken, but I picked up on it early.

I related to military stories in my family. My dad was named after a great-uncle in the Marine Corps who was gassed by the Germans in World War I. Uncle Larry came home wounded and died at an early age. He had an amazing amount of cancer that I'm sure was caused by the mustard gas. He had so much cancer that the University of California, Berkeley, asked to have his body for research.

My grandmother's brother fought with Patton in Africa and Italy and made it all the way to the Battle of the Bulge in Belgium. I had other relatives who served, too, and heard their stories as I was growing up. I just always wanted to be somebody who would stand up for what's right. I wanted to be part of that club.

My junior year, my dad and I went to meet with a Marine Corps recruiter, and the guy immediately tried to sign me up as a forward observer. When we left, Dad explained the job. I would be working independently behind enemy lines most of the time, with minimal support. Missions could last for days or weeks. But the Marine recruiter didn't tell me any of those details, so we kept looking.

The next guy was with the National Guard. I kind of liked the sound of the Army Reserves, and the unit was in Fort Pierce, about a twenty-five-minute drive from my home. I knew I could drill with the guys my senior year, then work one weekend a month and get full pay and benefits. My plan was to do the same through college. I enlisted, which took care of my immediate future—at least the next six years. My dad had to sign for me, since I wasn't eighteen.

Joining the National Guard in high school was pretty cool. There were three of us from my high school and two from the school across town who were active. Several others had signed up, but were delayed entry. We got to wear a lot of camouflage, march around in combat boots, get trained on all kinds of weapons, and do drills that simulated live fire. I knew the really hard part would come after my senior year—basic training (boot camp). But I didn't see how it could be any tougher than all my other jobs up to that point.

I've worked since I was a nine-year-old kid. I worked a lot of odd jobs around our rural home in Palm City, which is just north of Palm Beach in southeast Florida. I rode my dirt bike to a widow lady's barn, shoveled stalls, and exercised her horses, and I cashiered at my dad's coffee shop when he would let me. I drove a tractor in one-hundred-degree heat to mow grass in orange groves and hauled hundreds of gallons of chemicals to spray citrus. I used a machete to cut down vines around grapefruit trees. I was a laborer for sod farms, too. As someone else drove the tractor and cut the sod, I stacked it on pallets.

After school and some Saturdays, I worked with my buddy Kevin laying tile. His uncle owned the company, and we did the hard labor. After we ripped up carpet, I would haul five-gallon buckets of mud and fifty-pound boxes of tile while Kevin put them in place. It's what country kids did, worked blue-collar jobs. We were average looking—I was lanky, tall and skinny—not like body builders, but scrappy. We were what some people call "country strong." The jobs didn't pay well, but I managed to save enough to buy my first truck at age fifteen, before I was licensed to drive.

One of my more steady jobs in high school was working for a grove owned by Sunrise Citrus. My boss and his family lived in the middle of several thousand acres of orange and grapefruit trees that he managed. I learned a lot from him and thought maybe someday I'd manage a grove like he did. That was about the extent of my dreams of the future.

As hard as I had trained with the National Guard in high school, I came perilously close to missing Army basic training. The last semester of my senior year, I got really sick. You know that fever-with-chills, too-weak-to-stand-up kind of sick? The doctors couldn't figure out what was wrong with me. I was six feet tall and 170 pounds at normal weight, but dropped down to 135. I hardly left my house for three months.

There are two theories about what caused it. My mom thinks it was a disease I caught from exotic plants. At the time, one of my jobs was with a wholesale florist. I would drive two hours south to Miami and pick up a half a million dollars' worth of roses that had arrived on a plane from Ecuador. I would then bring them back to Martin County, where they would be transferred to other trucks and delivered to florists.

My theory is probably more accurate, but not as flattering. One night I did about twenty-four shots of Jim Beam. I'm serious: twenty-four. Someone later told me that Jim Morrison died on twenty-two shots, so I can't believe it didn't kill me. I completely blacked out, and somehow I ended up at the bottom of a pond. That's what my buddy Kevin Smith told me, since he was the one who waded out and brought me to shore. I got sick—violently. A couple of my friends put me in a garage, and when I woke up the next day, I didn't remember anything. It took me awhile to figure out where I was before I finally recovered enough to walk about a mile back to my house.

From that point on, I kept getting sicker. The doctor tested me for mono and the flu, and the symptoms were similar, but they couldn't confirm a diagnosis. I stayed home with fever and chills, and I kept losing weight. I couldn't work or train, and I was barely able to make it to our senior graduation ceremony at the football stadium. Afterward, everybody went to Project Graduation, a giant party where they take your keys and lock the seniors in an auditorium all night. But I went straight back to my house and climbed in bed, which was not like me. I stayed that way the entire summer, moving between the couch, the floor, and the bed. I could hardly hold my head up.

About three weeks out from the start of basic training, everyone thought I would have to bail. For one, I figured they would take one look at me, notice how much weight I'd lost, and think, "What, does this kid have cancer?"

I started to get back into training, bit by bit. But I was nowhere near where you need to be to face the ultimate endurance test. I packed my things and boarded a plane to Oklahoma, hoping for the best.

CHAPTER 3
Holy Terror

In the fall of 2000, I arrived at Fort Sill in Lawton, Oklahoma, where Army artillery soldiers are trained.

In the military, going through basic training is the first time you come face-to-face with your personal limit. It lasts nine weeks. You have to be pumped up, physically and mentally. I'd heard all the stories about drill instructors who would try to scare me. I thought, *I'm ready, I've seen the movies. Let's see what you've got.* Basic training would only be nine weeks, so I was thinking, *I can take it.* Guys I met those first few days told me much later, once they got to know me, that they'd wondered, *Who the heck is this skinny little kid with this damn mouth on him?* Even though I was only 135 pounds, I still had a 170-pound attitude.

Recruits arrive at Fort Sill together on a bus. When we pulled up to this waiting area, our bus was immediately surrounded. These men came out and started slamming the bus. It got really loud inside. And I thought, *OK, I've seen this in a movie.*

Then some guy got on the bus with this tortured look, like he was just pissed off. He was probably thirty, and we were about eighteen, and he was a big man. We were all cocky, dressed in our normal clothes from wherever we were from. The brothers were dressed one way. The white kids who listened to Guns N' Roses were dressed another way. Guys like me, I don't know; I guess I'm just a country boy. Everybody was so psyched up, because you've got to be pumped. But when this guy came onto the bus, we all shut down. I looked around at the gorillas outside, and I didn't want to so much as cough. I could tell some of the other guys were already scared. *Uh, oh, it's going to be a long time for you jokers. It's on, man. It has* started.

Then the big, angry guy informed us we had to get off the bus and get lined up. He gave us all these directions that nobody could remember. We got out there, and we failed. We got yelled at and screamed at. You know, the indoctrination started right away. You've got to do what you're told when you're told.

Then we were herded into a room and told to sit in these chairs, and they started a paperwork circle. Tons of paperwork. Our job was to be quiet and listen. This was the first time in my life I'd had to keep my mouth shut. Next thing I know, it's the next day. We had been doing things the whole time in that classroom, filling out forms mostly. On this one, it's last name first, first name, and middle initial. On the next one, it was first name, middle initial, then last name. You had to do it their way, even if it didn't make any sense. They wanted to know everything about us, *everything*—our life history. They would get us up and make us stand in formation and wait. Then it was back to filling out forms.

On day two, at least we were outside. It smelled a lot different than Florida. Really dry and dusty. The air was hot. We walked along concrete paths leading to different buildings. In the military, all of their stuff is perfect. There should not be a single blade of grass on the sidewalk. If somebody steps on the grass, they're screamed at. You could hear it a mile away, like the roar a gator makes in the swamp: "Get off *my* grass!" Whoever did it would be dead. They'd be there doing push-ups for*ever*.

When we got back to our barracks, we were completely wiped out. You're never sure how long you have. They always just say, "Until we come and get you." You may have just enough time to change your uniform, or they might let you sleep for two hours. This went on for three weeks. It's part of the brigade reception process, preparing recruits for the journey from civilian to soldier. It's what has to happen before the nine-week basic training even starts. The whole time they tell you, "They're going to kill you over there. You're not going to make it."

We got all pumped up to prove them wrong.

You get about thirty minutes once a week to go buy supplies, stuff you need, from a mini PX. They give you this huge list. With what time you have left, you frantically write letters home.

Looking back, I think, *What a bunch of wimps*, because basic training is the easiest thing you ever do in the military, but it's the hardest thing you've ever done at that point. Pretty early on, some guys in my group were already talking about quitting. You'd hear them say, "I want to get out of here. I can't take this." This was during the "Don't ask, don't tell" era, and one day, two guys went to the drill sergeant and said they were gay. He said, "Well, then kiss." They kissed and then boom, we never saw them again.

If you decide you want out, this is when you do it. Once you start the nine-week basic training, they really don't let you out. And once you get into the real Army, it's like prison. You're not getting out of there. So they kind of want you to get out if you're not ready, but they want it to happen at the indoctrination level.

The reception part was getting to me, too, but in a different way. I didn't sign up for doing all this prep stuff, paperwork, and standing around. It's hard to stay brave for three weeks, waiting to go across the tracks to get the real training started. When I left home, I thought it was going to be *on*. But three weeks in, our time had not even started.

Finally, the night before we were supposed to go over the tracks, none of us could sleep. The convoy pulled up that morning, and then—get this—they loaded us into cattle cars, the kind you see on semitrucks. And the guy behind the wheel was driving like an idiot. He was going around the curves so fast that guys were flying into each other and into the walls. Some of us were laughing; it was like a freaking amusement park ride. Some were scared, and others were getting pissed at the driver.

We started seeing obstacle courses. Then we saw grass and then mulch. Then we saw wooden signs with the names of the units. Each one was decorated with the unit's mascot, like the Wolfhounds or Hounds of Hell, probably drawn by a private with graphic design skills. As we went down the road, we'd see another sign, very official looking, but it was hard to understand what the signs meant because that world was so foreign to us.

The cattle cars took a sharp right and pulled into an individual training area with a three-story building labeled 1/40, first of the fortieth. There were thirty drill sergeants waiting under a breezeway. Not *one* this time, but thirty. They ran out and started beating the crap out of the cattle car and screaming. Finally, they told us to come out of the trailer. Then they just screamed and screamed. Our guys started running around trying to follow commands. The drill sergeants yelled, "Grab your bag. Put it on this line." "Grab that bag." Our guys looked dazed from all the screaming.

Finally, we managed to get the bags in order, and someone said, "We're going to call your name. You're going to go to this spot." Boom, there goes the first platoon, roughly thirty men. My buddies Tim Baltes and Mark Allen, who would be in my unit back at Fort Pierce, got assigned to a different platoon than me. I thought, *How did I get sent over here and they're both together?*

When you're assigned to your platoon, for the first time you're with "your guys." These are going to be guys that you live with, train with, fight with, like, love, and then someday you're going to say, "We're going to be best buds. I'll call you," and of course no one ever calls.

My squad leader was Staff Sergeant Riggins. He was big, mean, and loud. He had this raspy southern accent. He'd say, "How's it going today?" in a type of scream. He was hard to understand, but you didn't dare let on because then he would get in your face.

It was a real show. We were all scared to death. We got very little sleep and we had to learn an incredible number of details. For example, one of the first things they do is show you where to store your stuff. They yell, "This is a wall locker!" And I'm thinking, *Okay, this is going to be easy.* Then it starts. "From the left, you're going to have your Class-A uniform jacket, and then two inches to the right—*exactly two inches*—you will have your pants to the Class-A uniform." I thought, *Oh, wow, this isn't going to be easy* at all. It literally takes all day to learn how to set up the wall locker. We've got the jacket and then the pants and then the Class-A shirt. Then the white T-shirts. Done, that's it.

Just when I thought, *Okay. We're good now,* they show you how to organize the drawer. T-shirts are smoothed out and rolled tight. Then you've got your socks, and they have to be rolled just so. We had a whole class on how to roll them with a smiley face. And those smiley faces had better be smiling. Then there was underwear. There's a class on underwear! Then we got to the wool socks and the dress socks. That's another drawer. And that drawer is to be opened two inches at all times. The next drawer was to be opened four, then six, all for easy inspection. You go through the exercise until every piece of your uniform is in there, and this takes for*ever*. And don't think you're done, because they will come by at all times of the night and day and push over your wall locker. So now what would require about three days' worth of work, you'll have to get done in about three minutes. Everything has a sense of urgency, and unrealistic timeframes are the norm.

You just always fail. Fail, fail, fail. That's what they want, and then they start to build you up again. If you dare to answer, you'll hear, "You don't know. Shut up." If you mess up at all, they might take you out back and smoke you with push-ups, squats, mountain climbers for hours. Just torture. Tensions are high, and some guys end up in fistfights. When a drill sergeant finally comes in, there could be blood everywhere.

But that's all part of it. They want you to get tired. They want you to get beat up. They want you to beat on each other. They want leaders to emerge. It just happens. You don't see it; you're in such a panic mode. You get three minutes to call home on Sunday, a privilege you might lose if someone screws up. You want to talk to your girlfriend. You want to brush your teeth whenever you like or go to the bathroom whenever you like—it doesn't matter. You have absolutely no freedom. Everything that is American is gone now.

That first week, you learn about your weapon and how to take it apart. In the military, you're only as good as your weakest guy, you're only as good as your leadership, and you're only as good as your trust in each other and in your weapon. And you'll never have confidence in your weapon if you don't understand every working part. I've owned guns since I was twelve years old, but I never thought about why they work, I just knew they would. In the military, the weapon became an extension of me. I could throw a punch and hit you at three feet, but a pistol gave me thirty feet of range. A rifle gave me a thousand feet.

That's what we were learning: you *are* the weapon, and you've got to become familiar and confident in both. You can't have confidence in your weapon if you don't understand every working part. So we started with how to take it apart and why. We learned what each part does and how it functions, so if you have a jam or a problem on the battlefield, you can clear it quickly. If it's broken, knowing the working parts will help you identify where the problem is to save time with the armor repair shop. You have to know your weapon; you've got to clean it and take care of it. It may just be the thing that keeps you and your friends alive.

They didn't say it, but everything was, *We're going to teach you, then we're going to beat you down, then we'll feed you, then we'll teach you and beat you down, then feed you. We'll give you, like, an hour to sleep. Then we'll teach you and beat you down.* This went on and on that first week.

During week two, we learned how to march. That is, out on the asphalt during the hottest part of the day, when it was ninety-five degrees. Hot. We were in four lines, one behind the other, in formation. We learned how to hold our weapons and make uniformly timed and sweeping movements in drill and ceremonies. If somebody did something wrong, we had to start the drill over. They added variety with push-ups. Endless push-ups. Your palms get raw from doing push-ups on hot asphalt. My hands had built up callouses over the years from throwing hay bales and working on the tractor, which helped a little, but not much. My feet became bruised and raw.

Everyone does the exercises—there are no exceptions. Even if you're planning to be a cook or a mail guy in the Army, you march and do push-ups. I had signed up to be an Air Defender, an Avenger crewmember. My job would be to shoot fast movers out of the sky—jets and helicopters—which sounds glamorous, but it didn't really feel like it while I was marching for what felt like forever and doing endless push-ups.

CHAPTER 4

My Heisman Moment

I had been waiting for basic rifle marksmanship training since my first day, when we were doing all the paperwork. One of the drill sergeants who was trying to look mean, but was really kind of dumpy, asked, "Who here is from West Virginia?" Two hands out of about seventy went up. And the mean dumpy-looking sergeant said, "You guys look to them on week four, basic rifle marksmanship. Them boys from West Virginia can shoot."

I looked to the back of the room, and the two West Virginia dudes were grinning, like, *Yeah, you heard him.* That kind of pissed me off. I remember thinking, *Who the hell are you? Shooting is shooting. It doesn't matter where you're from. My dad is a Marine, and he taught me how to shoot, so we'll see what happens.*

Since we finally knew how to march after what was easily 150 hours of practice, that's how week four started: We marched to the range. We were given M16 rifles, a weapon I had never fired before. It was the first one I had ever touched. Everyone and their brother has an AR-15 now, but this was in 2000, before the military weapon craze.

On the M16, the sights are just a peephole at the back of the weapon, and I was used to regular open sights like on a BB gun, hunting rifle, or pistol. My .30-30 Winchester and .22 rifle both have definite measuring. On those, I've got a tiny little bead that fits in a V-shaped notch perfectly, and I can shoot the eye out of a bird with it. Besides the sights, the M16 also had a ten-pound trigger, which is a really tough pull. The Army doesn't want you shooting this thing unless you mean to kill.

The drill sergeants instructed us on the weapon. We were told, "You've got to rest your cheek on the butt of the rifle the same way every time because you have to zero to that." Your nose rests against the cold metal of the charging handle, which isn't comfortable, but it's the only way to get consistency.

I couldn't believe what I was hearing. I was like, *You guys have had this since Vietnam? Don't we have something better since Vietnam?* Anyway, I was a little nervous and kept thinking this thing couldn't be accurate at all.

But at the range, I do what I'm told—exactly what I'm told. I ended up shooting a really tight shot at twenty-five meters to get my weapon zeroed to me. Then the next day we marched out again four to five miles. To familiarize ourselves with the weapon, we shot human silhouette full-torso targets at twenty-five and then fifty meters. I was getting used to it, but I still didn't like the way the weapon pounded against my face. And when you fired, the charging handle jolted the end of your nose, so you had to concentrate on not flinching and screwing up your aim.

The third or fourth day of that week, it was time to qualify. We were all nervous, wondering how we were going to do. We marched with our weapons, pointing them straight in front of us like we were going in ready to kill somebody. We all maintained the same position while the drill sergeant screamed at us. You've got to learn how to be comfortable with your weapon while working in highly uncomfortable surroundings.

We didn't know the course but were told there would be forty targets. We were given forty bullets and would be tested for speed and accuracy. When it was my turn to qualify, I checked to make sure the weapon was cleared. Then the drill instructor hit me on the back and said, "Go!" I walked as fast as I could—safely—there's no running on the range. A guy in the tower was screaming into a microphone and there were eyes everywhere.

I walked quickly to lane 7 and lowered myself into the concrete foxhole, which was about five or six feet deep. Across the range, which was about three football fields long, I saw a plastic silhouette target, just the torso. The drill sergeant assigned to my hole and two other holes was pacing. If you did something unsafe, they would be on you like a hornet. They would run up and kick you in the face, knock you out. The range is a hands-on environment because of the weapons. They're not supposed to put their hands on you and hurt you anywhere else on the base, but on the range, we're fair game. Everyone's armed, so if they think you're going to do something, you're going down. Everyone's shooting at once. It's a pretty stressful backdrop.

It was finally time to shoot. The first targets were fast ready at fifteen meters away. Everything in the military is meters. The football fans would ask, "What about that fifty-yard…"and a drill sergeant would scream, "Meters! Listen, you little redneck, it's meters!"

So the fifty-meter half-torso fast ready target would pop up and hold for about two seconds and then go down. Then the next one came up for a few seconds, and then he went down. Then the hundred-meter target would hold for maybe five seconds and then disappear. The 150-meter target followed for six seconds. It kept going like that until the target was out to three hundred yards, and that might be up for about ten seconds. Between pulls, you try to find that rhythm. The ideal is to exhale and squeeze the trigger right at the bottom of that natural pause between breaths. But when you're out there trying to qualify, you've got these things popping up and down and people yelling at you and all the eyes watching you, and it's like, *Good luck finding that rhythm.*

But somehow, I managed to find it.

When I got in the foxhole, I blocked out everything. I wanted to win. I *really* wanted to win. I charged my weapon and it was *go* time. It was the most focused I'd ever been in my life. I was done with all this ridicule. I was done hearing about those two West Virginia jokers who were going to blow everybody's butt away.

The targets started coming up, and I hit them. I aimed very small, very center. I was so focused. I felt like I had the best vision of my life that day. I was just *pow, pow, pow.* At the end, I knew I'd gotten them all. It was my Heisman friggin' moment.

I had been hearing the reports earlier in the day, like "Lane 6: thirty-six out of forty. Congratulations, expert." And, "Lane 1: twenty-seven out of forty." That was barely a marksman. Years later, I was in the infantry, where everybody had to be an "expert." They make you sit out there for days until you can do it. It's your *job.* But this was still early; we were not even trained yet. I was sitting there waiting for the tower to confirm. They got to my number. "Lane 7: forty out of forty."

It was like I had thrown the winning touchdown pass.

Everybody looked around. There hadn't been a perfect score all day. I came off the range, and my buddies from home, who were in the other platoon together, came running up to me. "Did you shoot forty out of forty?" I was like, "Yeah."

They couldn't believe it. "What, did you have extra bullets?" I said, "No!" They still did not believe it. And the rest of the day, I kept hearing the question, "Who shot forty out of forty?" It was like one of those videos that goes viral on the Internet. Everybody was talking about it.

My dad had given me some advice when I first joined the military: "Never be first and never be last—be in the center." I'd pretty much followed that rule. Even when we went on a run and the drill sergeants would speed up to see who would fall out, I did not try to take them on:

Yeah, I can hang. Yeah, I'm Luke Murphy. Because I knew they would ride me if I did too well, I'd always tried to stay near the center.

And here I was right out in the front, an easy target. Uh-oh.

Thankfully, it didn't turn out that way. My drill sergeant, Riggins, started claiming his own victory. He said I'd shot well because of his training. I'm thinking, *Dude, no way,* but to his face, I said, "Yup, it's your training there."

We had to march four miles back to our barracks, and I tell you, I didn't feel my bruised feet at all on the way home. I was on cloud nine. There must have been some talk between my squad leader and his higher-up, because the next thing you know, a drill sergeant came to me and said, "Tomorrow when we go back to the range, you're going to stay behind, because you've already qualified. We're going to give you a four-hour pass to go wherever you want." I was wondering, *Is this a good thing?* And then I realized this was a *very* good thing.

That next day, I went to Taco Bell. I never ate fast food growing up, but for some reason, because I could do anything I wanted, I went to Taco Bell. I ordered whatever I felt like having. Then I went to the PX and bought a calling card and called everybody at home. I thought about those guys who had the four-mile march out to the range and back. They were out there getting yelled at, trying to shoot again, wondering how the hell I'd hit forty out of forty. I went back to the barracks and there was nobody around. I took a nap. They had only given me four hours, but it felt like four days.

My platoon wasn't back from the range by dinner, so I went to chow hall alone. I passed a drill sergeant marching a mixed bag of Army artillery guys and Marine artillery guys. "Left, left, left…" and then, "Halt!" I could feel him sizing me up, this little punk, alone, no patch on my arm. Just a dumb fish out there flopping, about to get eaten.

He came right up to my face and said, "Where are you supposed to be?" I answered in one breath: "Drill Sergeant, I-shot-forty-out-of-forty-on-the-range-yesterday-and-they-gave-me the-day-off."

He looked at me and laughed. "Well, hot damn, hawkeye. Carry on."

I did an about-face and decided, *I am going back to my freaking room, and I'm gonna wait there. I'm not risking getting eaten again.* At least I had answered the question right for a change.

CHAPTER 5
The Enemy from Within

We made it through the nine weeks of basic training, and everyone called home to tell their family members about graduation. My family doesn't really have that one person that you call, who tells everyone else, which meant I had to call them individually. They all asked, "Does that mean you want us to come to graduation?" I said, "Well, do whatever you want to do." My girlfriend at the time was at school in Florida, and the graduation would be in Oklahoma. My family didn't have a lot of money, and hers didn't, either, so I knew it would be difficult for them to attend. When I called my dad, he said, "Nobody came to my graduation." That kind of decided it.

When graduation day arrived, everybody's family was there. *Everybody's* family. Baltes and Allen from back home had their parents and siblings. And because my family wasn't there, I had to do extra duty, while everyone else went out to dinner with their girlfriends and moms and dads, sisters and brothers. I thought, *Great, if you don't have family, you get punished?*

One of my buddies, Matt, had his family there, and I was going to sneak off with them, until I heard Drill Sergeant Riggins. "Murphy! Get over here. You ain't got no family." And minutes later, there I was with a mop in my hand.

From Fort Sill, we were going straight to school to learn our jobs. For me, that was ten weeks of Air Defense Artillery School in Fort Bliss, Texas. On the flight to El Paso, we had a stopover at Wichita Falls. The next flight was overbooked, and they asked if anyone wanted to stay behind and get a voucher. They needed two of us, and I raised my hand. "I'll stay. I'll take some money." It ended up being five hundred dollars of free travel. I was like, *All right, Christmas! I'm going home, you suckers. And you get to be yelled at first.*

Bad idea. Really bad idea.

I stayed back with a kid named Walker. He had been in the platoon with my buddies, Baltes and Allen, in basic training. Walker was one of those guys who would fight, and he was a Golden Glove boxer, so he would just tear suckers up. These were not fair fights. Fighting Walker was like fighting your dad when you're six years old. He'd get in this old-school boxing stance. His left foot would be pointed at you and his right foot would be parallel behind it. Then he'd come at you like this Irish pirate. He could breathe into his jabs, and within three shots, people were bleeding and done.

So I stayed back with Walker, and he was cocky. He was kind of standoffish at first, and then he warmed up to me. By the time we got the next flight four hours later, we were almost buddies, listening to different music together.

While we were at the airport, I bought a *Maxim* magazine to kill time. It's got girls in bikinis, eating tips, what's cool to wear—man stuff. Probably some of the same sex tips they've put in every issue, but it's not porno. I stuffed it in my bag. When we got to Fort Bliss around eleven that night, everybody was in bed except for the drill sergeant. There's always one awake. Walker and I were loaded down with our bags and saw this muscular guy coming toward us wearing a tucked-in brown T-shirt. He was probably thirty years old. "Who are you two fairies?" he said.

We answered him. "Private Murphy, Drill Sergeant." "Private Walker, Drill Sergeant." We told him the plane was overbooked and we had to come later. "I know that. I've been waiting for you idiots. Dump your shit out."

We dumped our bags on the ground. This was shaping up to be like basic training. I was surprised; I thought the school part was supposed to be better.

The drill sergeant saw the *Maxim* magazine and got right up in my face. "What are you, some kind of pervert?"

I tried to answer without sarcasm, "No, Drill Sergeant."

He said, "Oh, yeah, you've got this nudie magazine." I'm thinking, *It's a* Maxim, *dude. I guarantee you it's not contraband.* But I stayed quiet.

"Why don't you do some push-ups there, pervert." My new nightmare had begun. I got down and started doing push-ups. I was tired and sweating, and finally I couldn't do any more. He barked, "Do some mountain climbers." I started into those grueling plank exercises for another few minutes, and I could see Walker—tough guy—standing there looking pretty nervous, like, *What have we done?*

Pretty soon, the drill sergeant asked Walker, "Why don't you join him?"

Next the drill sergeant had us do sit-ups. Finally, he allowed us to get up and put our bags back together again. I did it as fast as possible because I couldn't wait to get away from this guy. I wanted to go to bed and this was crap. Over a *Maxim*! I never should have bought that dumb magazine. I'd never even read it before.

By the time we got our lockers set up—remember the locker drill?—it was probably three in the morning, and we had to be up at five thirty.

The next day, I thought there was no way that drill sergeant would remember me. I'd given him what he wanted, and besides, there were six hundred new guys there they had to train. As I walked back from the chow hall after breakfast, I heard, "Hey, pervert." I'm like, *Oh my god, it's the dude with the thing about* Maxim. And I had ten weeks to go.

* * *

The first couple of weeks went by, and the running was tougher. It was a lot faster than basic training, where we ran at about an eight–or nine-minute per mile pace. But here, they had a fast group, medium group, and slow group. The fast group easily ran a seven-minute pace. They slowed down, to an eight-minute mile once in a while. The medium group ran about a seven-thirty pace, which is what you need to pass. You've got to run two seven-thirty miles just to pass. I knew I could do seven-minute miles, so I volunteered for the fast group. I figured if you were in the fast group, maybe you wouldn't be called "pervert." It came with other perks, too: if you were in the fast group, after two weeks you were allowed to move to "permanent party," and you got certain privileges, like free nights.

My buddies Baltes and Allen were also in the fast group. After two weeks, the two of them were assigned permanent party, but for some reason my name wasn't called. I thought, *Whoa. I've got no deficiencies. I've been in the fast group—I volunteered!* I went over and asked the drill sergeant, who confirmed my name wasn't on the sheet. He referred me to someone else, who said, "No, you're name's not here." Then that guy referred me to—you guessed it—the *Maxim* drill sergeant.

I walked up and *Maxim* said, "Hey, pervert."

I said, "Drill Sergeant, with all due respect, I'm not on the list for permanent party."

He shot back, "And you're not going to be, not as long as I'm here." So I had six more weeks of drudgery while my buddies lived it up. Relatively speaking.

The *Maxim* incident wasn't my only trouble at Fort Bliss. I stumbled into another trap that cost me an Article 15, a "nonjudicial punishment" for any number of offenses and one of the worst things you can get in the Army. It goes on your permanent record. And I got it for buying a protein workout supplement from the PX.

I can still hear the drill sergeant's accusation, "What have you got here? What have you got? Oh, you think you can take this?" I was still trying to get back to my normal weight, and it wasn't like it was a banned substance, plus it wasn't even opened yet. The PX is the base store, so if we can't have it, why would they sell it?

At the time, I looked to the drill sergeants like they were John Wayne. I thought they were the toughest guys I'd ever meet. In reality, I know a lot of them have a chip on their shoulder. Some have problems. I didn't know that at the time, which didn't help much.

They sent me to this freaking room for a minitrial. It was dark with camo netting. I saw this sandbag wall and a sandbag desk. Behind the camo curtain was a captain. He barked, "Come here. Sit down." He read off all these charges, trying to scare me. He shoved a piece of paper in my face and growled, "Sign here." I signed it. *Whatever, dude. Stupid protein. My buddies are on permanent party, and I'm still stuck over here at the back. I'm in the fast group. Screw this!* I walked out with my Article 15 and my sentence: two weeks cleaning latrines.

Finally, after weeks and weeks of learning how to shoot down enemy Scud missiles, planes, and helicopters, and learning some other secret stuff, it was time for graduation. Again.

And once again, families came. Not mine.

At this point, I was starting to get a little broken down. I just wanted to get out of there, to go back home and report to the National Guard unit and do my weekend assignments, whatever. That drill sergeant had been riding me for months, and I was *done*. After the ceremony, I was heading out to catch my flight back to Florida when the drill sergeant—that idiot—found me. He found me!

He asked me to go do something. *Dude, I graduated*, I thought. *Sure, I am still in the Army, but*…He asked me if I had five ranks, if I was an E6, staff sergeant. Of course I wasn't. I was a private. I went ahead and did what he asked, and then he asked me to do something else. I answered, "No, drill sergeant. I have a flight to catch." He started screaming at me. Then I had to do push-ups. I saw my buddies leaving in taxis, going to the airport, and there I was getting friggin' destroyed by this lunatic.

Finally, it was about twenty minutes before my flight, and *Maxim* finally gave me back my airline ticket. I could see the airport across the desert, so I grabbed my long green canvas bag and threw it over my shoulder. I was wearing wool Class-A greens and shiny black shoes with dress socks, but I didn't care. I just started booking it across the field. I made it to the flight right before they closed the doors.

I slumped in the seat. And as the plane took off, I felt like I had survived a war.

Anyone who has gone through basic training will tell you it's torture. But compared to war, it's the weakest thing ever. Still, I never thought I would get ridden the whole time. Even my buddies, Baltes and Allen, said they felt bad seeing what that guy did to me. I'd been a tough kid growing up; I didn't get bullied. It's not cool to be bullied, but I think it makes you tougher.

I had never been the unlucky one. To this day, I cannot look at a *Maxim* magazine.

CHAPTER 6
Mission to the Future

In training, somebody has got to be the bad guy, what we call the OP-4 (opposing force). In the spring before 9/11, it was my turn. I volunteered for a mission to test the recently enhanced Apache Longbow helicopter. Me and some other guys would hide in the desert, and the pilots would try to kill us, while we would try to shoot the bird down with a Stinger missile. Pretty exciting stuff for a twenty-year-old. I flew from Florida to Texas for the assignment.

I knew a little about the Longbow, which had only been around since 1997. The combat helicopter was able to pick up heat and movement and other vital details at a safer range. The pilot could see the element on a tiny screen, and he could decide whether or not to fire without ever being exposed. At the time I thought, *Man, how lazy are these pilots?* They don't even have to find what they're aiming at anymore. It's all done for them and put in front of their noses.

We arrived at Fort Bliss and they immediately briefed us. They gave us coordinates on a grid—a place on the map—and it was up to us to find our way. We loaded up our gear, including camouflage to cover the vehicles, and drove our Humvees into the desert. We were in a very remote, highly classified area where top-secret missions played out. I kept seeing remnants of old rounds along the way. We got into our positions and waited. I started thinking how cool it was to get a shot at killing a Longbow. I figured the Apache pilots were probably sitting back in their barracks, watching *Top Gun* and thinking how cool they were, too.

As it grew dark, the temperature dropped and the quiet settled over us like a blanket. I started hearing animal-type sounds that I'd never heard before. People were always reporting UFOs in that part of the country, and now I know why, because I thought I was seeing them.

Around midnight, I heard something that sounded like a big-ass mosquito. I looked around and thought, *What in the world?* I saw this black object in the air coming toward us—maybe the size of a kid's model airplane. It hung in the air momentarily, then turned around.

About an hour later, I heard the Apache. I was getting ready, getting into position, and then got a call saying we were dead.

What?

"Yeah, they killed you from four thousand meters out."

I thought, *Are you kidding me? That's not even fair.* That was a couple of miles away, you know? But the mission was over.

When we got back to debrief, they told us that big-ass mosquito was a drone—it was one of the earliest versions, and at the time we'd never heard of them. It took our picture and gave our exact location to the pilot, so they eliminated us without giving themselves away.

They wanted to repeat the exercise during daylight the next day. We headed out to a different place and got into position, but the same darn thing happened: they nailed us. I thought, *What good is this training?* You tell us to go to a spot, then send a drone out to that spot to take our picture. The drone goes back and tells the pilot, "Yup, there's the spot." The helicopter stays hidden and shoots us—game over.

We were going to repeat the exercise the next evening, and I got a great idea. I went to the assigned spot at first. We had been told exactly where to go; they didn't want us moving around too much because there's a lot of unexploded ordnance in the area and it could be dangerous. Besides, it's not a good idea to disobey direct orders. But

I decided to move about seventy-five yards closer to some big desert rocks. I had about ten gallons of water with me, so I poured water on the vehicle to cool off the heat signature. I took the manpack (weapon) and moved it another fifty yards from where I was supposed to be and sat down to wait.

About an hour later, I heard that stupid little drone coming. After it turned to head back, I jumped in the Humvee and moved it, then poured more water on it. I got the manpack and I moved that, too.

I saw the Apache Longbow approaching, headed for where the drone had found us. Since the pilot didn't see me, he was forced to come closer. I saw him circling around looking for the dummy he was supposed to kill. When he got into range, I popped out from behind a rock and locked onto him with my Stinger missile. He never saw me.

The button I pushed determines if the aircraft is friend or foe by a series of beeps. If the Longbow had been a real enemy, then I would pull the trigger and the Stinger missile would shoot out about twenty-eight feet before igniting the rocket. (If the rocket ignited right off the end of the Stinger tube, it would burn a soldier's face off.) Since I was using a simulated weapon, the missile didn't launch.

But I killed him—virtually. I was so happy.

Unfortunately, the leadership wasn't as thrilled. When I got back, they told me I had not obeyed the rules. My job was to go out there and get killed. I couldn't help it, though. Sometimes my competitive nature just takes over.

The next day they did an after-action review, but the OP-4s weren't invited—of course. It was only for the cool-guy officers. Later, me and the other "bad guys" were at chow hall, and some men came in dressed in flight suits. Somebody said, "Hey, those are the pilots we've been going up against." When I turned around to look, I realized they were not what I was expecting. I wanted to see someone like

Tom Cruise, or really cool-looking dudes sporting aviator sunglasses. It never crossed my mind that they could look like average guys or dorks. You know, really smart guys —way smarter than me at the time. I had this stereotype in my mind of what they would look like, based on Hollywood, I guess.

I said something sarcastic to one of the pilots, and boy, he said something really smartass right back at me. Reality check: He was an officer and I was a nobody. I told myself, *Okay, better let it go, or you'll end up losing that battle.* It was one of the few times I was able to hold my tongue.

* * *

After September 11, I did eventually get the call I had expected, but it wasn't specific. It was more like, *We're putting you on notice so you can figure out what to do with your college classes, because we're pretty sure you're going somewhere.*

All my buddies were up at our National Guard unit in Fort Pierce cleaning weapons. They had the place locked down. The country was really uncertain what to expect. Nobody knew how big 9/11 was going to get. We knew the plane that went down in Pennsylvania had targeted the White House, and both the Pentagon and the World Trade Center had been hit. But nobody knew how complex the thing was.

Every US airport went on high alert, and the National Guard was put in charge of guarding them. I ended up dropping my classes and volunteering to go to an airport. I was immediately assigned to Miami International, a hundred miles south.

That's where I met guys from all over the state who were in different National Guard units. I met soldiers who had been active duty and in the infantry and some who had been on missions in Bosnia. Others had been to Somalia and would tell us their version of the events portrayed in the movie *Black Hawk Down*. While I was on assignment in Miami, I learned more about the military through their stories of combat.

Our shifts at the airport lasted ten hours. We stood there in our camo dress uniforms with a soft cap, which is a baseball hat with a camo pattern, and rifles.

You never knew how people were going to react. It's not every day in the US that you have soldiers in camo carrying M16s and 9mm pistols in the airport. One married couple told us they'd had a bet over whether our weapons were loaded. I dropped a magazine out and showed them my bullets. The wife acted kind of appalled, but her husband said, "Told ya!" I couldn't understand why she'd think we'd stand there with weapons that weren't loaded. That wouldn't scare off Al-Qaeda.

We sat at a checkpoint and backed up the Transportation Security Administration (TSA) agents. We had a lot of celebrities come through who didn't think they should be screened as hard as others. They would give the TSA agents hell, and when we walked up, they immediately changed their attitude. There were other VIPs who were cool and posed for pictures with us. We met Don Shula and got to see his 1972 Super Bowl ring. And one afternoon we rushed Michael Jordan after he'd just played the Miami Heat. He held up his huge hands in front of him, not sure what we were after with our weapons and uniforms, but later posed for photos.

Some people would thank us. Some acted really nervous. There were others who tested us, thinking we didn't have any authority. They found out the hard way that yeah, we could do things. Not the least of which was delaying them long enough that they would miss their flight.

For the first time in my life, I was actually making pretty good money, way more than the six-dollar-an-hour grind in an orange grove. These were regular hours, and I was getting paid every two weeks.

But when we weren't doing that, we were back at the Embassy Suites. I had the perfect shift—ten a.m. to eight p.m. After being at the airport all day, we'd shower, then go out on the town. I was from the cattle and citrus country in South Florida. The biggest city near my home was West Palm Beach, and that's not huge. It's no Miami, for sure. I found out pretty quickly that those Hispanic girls didn't want anything to do with a skinny white boy from the woods who had no money and drove a ratty old pickup truck. When we'd go to a club that required valet parking, I saw a different world. It was my first time seeing Ferraris and Maseratis. The other guys had to tell me what that shiny, sweet-looking red car was. It was total culture shock—completely different from where I grew up.

CHAPTER 7
It's War, and I'm Going Regular Army

I ended up doing six months at Miami International. I liked it, I really liked it. Obviously, it was nothing like real active duty would be, but doing it every day was so much better than once a month on a weekend.

Talking to all the guys who had been active duty planted a seed in me that kept growing. We watched as the Global War on Terror launched with Operation Enduring Freedom in Afghanistan on October 7, 2001. I was especially interested in how the 101st Airborne was destroying the terrorist training camps. It was having an effect. I started wondering if the National Guard was going to be enough for me.

My girlfriend at the time, Kristine, was beginning her freshman year at Florida State University, my dad's alma mater. I had been an FSU fan my whole life, but my dad gave Kristine an FSU charm that his dad had given him. He gave it to *her*! He didn't think any of his four sons would ever make it to FSU since we weren't the best students in high school. When I went up to visit, I could tell Kristine was having a great time, hanging out with sorority girls and enjoying the social life. I was a little jealous, but I started seeing a difference between guys like me and the ones at college. I felt like my calling was the military.

But what would an Army career look like?

After 9/11, the military budget was huge and there were a lot of job openings. I knew if I went active duty, I could pretty much pick any job I wanted. When you enlist in the Army, you have to take an Armed Services Vocational Aptitude Battery (ASVAB) test. How you score determines whether or not you can join and also determines what Military Occupational Specialties (MOS) you are eligible for in your Army career. In the National Guard, I had been trained as an Air Defender, a 14-S, which is the Avenger crew member. My role was to shoot enemy aircraft out of the sky. But now that I was into the military world, I realized it was unlikely I would ever get to do my job—there's just not a lot of need for it. And you don't run all those miles and do all the training to be ineffective.

I wanted to be in the fight. I wanted to be the best trained I could be, and that meant infantry.

To me, infantry was the most challenging job you could do. Nobody in their right mind should *want* to do it, really. I mean, you're going to have the worst time and the hardest job. For example, artillery guys load up artillery and shoot it toward a target. They radio back, "Yeah, we got a few." But they're not up front engaging one-on-one like infantry. They're not the ones always in the field training. They're not the guys running the most miles and staying fit and maintaining their expert status in marksmanship. Those are the things I was missing being in the National Guard as an Air Defender.

In the Army, anybody who is not infantry is called a POAG (Person Other Than a Grunt, a grunt being an Infantryman). It rhymes with "rogue." It's kind of a derogatory thing. Sometimes if you call an artillery guy a POAG, he'll tell you, "I'm not a POAG. I'm in combat arms." But infantry guys will tell you everybody is a POAG if they're not infantry. It's kind of like how Marines are always bragging. That's all they've got. It's one of the reasons you join the Marines, so you can *say* you're a Marine. There's no glory in it. It's a terrible job, just like being in the army infantry, but you can be proud of it.

I was done with the Miami assignment, so I told my leadership in the National Guard that I wanted to go to Army active duty. They were like, "Whoa, Luke. You owe us four more years." But I had already looked into it and knew I could transfer right in.

I went to talk to an Army recruiter and told him my scenario. Of course, he was all over me. The next thing you know, he's got paperwork for me to sign to make it official. In no time, I found myself in front of the colonel for the National Guard. He said, "You want go active duty?"

I said, "Yes, sir."

He extended his hand, and I met it with mine. "Done. Good luck."

My stomach was in my throat.

I called Kristine to tell her, and she was not thrilled. I told my family and Kristine's family. Then I called some of my buddies and their dads, who had been active-duty soldiers. I remember one of them, a retired Marine, saying, "Luke, do you know what you're getting yourself into, buddy?"

Of course I didn't. How could you know if you've never been?

One of the things the recruiter told me was that I could choose any major infantry unit. I had to think long and hard on that one. I wanted to be in a unit that I could be very proud of, so I started studying all the Army units and what they did.

On the Miami assignment, I met guys from all over—from the 101st Airborne in Kentucky, the Twenty-Fifth Infantry Tropic Lightning in Hawaii, and the Tenth Mountain Division in New York State. I recognized their shoulder patches. For example, the 101st is famous for the screaming eagle insignia. The Tenth Mountain design is two crossed bayonets that form an X. I may not know all of the patches, but I know the ones from the badass units. And I recognize combat patches. Seriously, think back to General Patton and what his uniform must have looked like—covered with patches. Think back to Audie Murphy, the most decorated American soldier of World War II. He had every military combat award for valor available from the US Army. My grandpa and other close relatives fought in that war, and I know those patches.

I started thinking about which unit might be a good fit for me. The Tenth Mountain Division, obviously, did a lot of mountain training, a lot of light infantry. At the time they were up at Fort Drum, New York, and I didn't want to go up there, mainly because it's cold and I'm a Florida boy. The Twenty-Fifth Infantry Tropic Lightning in Hawaii is very famous. But the work is not as glamorous as it sounds. Those guys are in mountainous jungle with lots of things that'll stab you and grab you when you walk around at night. Jungle training is relentless. Plus, I'd already had the beach. I know that Florida and Hawaii are very different, but in my opinion, beach is beach.

I looked at the Army's two airborne units. The 173rd Airborne is in Italy, and the Eighty-Second Airborne Division is in Fort Bragg, North Carolina, near Fayetteville. Of course, there's the 101st Airborne, but they don't jump anymore. It's really air assault, but you can't shake the name.

The Eighty-Second Airborne Division still jumps, but they go a long time between combat jumps. At that point, their last jump was into Panama (First Brigade Task Force) in 1989. Jumping from planes is just not an effective way of getting into combat because you can take fire and have to jump before you're supposed to, and that means the map you've memorized is no longer valid. Then I thought, *If they drop me into Iraq or Afghanistan and I break my leg, how the hell do I get out?*

At least with the 101st, you come in on a helicopter, and if something goes wrong, they can come back and get you. Unlike with a plane, which has to have a place to land. To me, helicopters seem to be the most efficient way to get into combat and get the job done. When you come in on a helicopter, you can see what's waiting for you when you hit the ground.

They've also got firepower—big guns on the side of the birds. So with the 101st, not only can you hit the ground fighting, you hit the ground and you know where you are because of the GPS coordinates.

I also took into consideration the history of the different units. There's a lot of pride in each unit's history. I wanted to go to a unit with a good reputation, because those usually have solid financing behind them and a bold attitude.

Then there was my desire to stay in the Southeast, which ruled out the 173rd in Italy. I've always been a country boy and a southerner. The 101st Airborne Division is located in Fort Campbell on the Tennessee and Kentucky border, and those states are gorgeous. The 101st units did different things in the war and were making a name for themselves at that time in Afghanistan. They were sought out in those major initial battles, including Operation Anaconda, which involved an intense firefight with Al-Qaeda and Taliban forces in the mountains of eastern Afghanistan. And if there was going to be a big mission, like Iraq, I wanted to be with a unit that was going to have some major involvement.

I called the recruiter back and told him I'd made my decision: I wanted the 101st Airborne Division.

The next time I heard from the military, it was through a letter giving me a date to report to Fort Benning for basic training. Yes, I had to go back to basic training. Infantry basic training is fourteen weeks, not nine like all other specialties in the regular Army. So I owed them another five weeks, which was kind of a nightmare, because I knew what I was getting into this time. It would have been great if they'd just teach me what I needed to know when I got to the 101st. But of course, that's not possible. So the plan was for me to show up to a unit that was already nine weeks into basic training and do the last few weeks with them. The adventure was about to start.

CHAPTER 8
Choosing the Rakkasans

When I arrived at Fort Benning in Columbus, Georgia, I was at the rank of corporal, which is an E4. But the higher-ups said, "You're not a corporal." I tried to explain, "Yes, I am, because I have been promoted three times." They said I had to be a specialist because corporal is a leadership position, and I was there to learn, not lead. Somehow, though, they forgot to take the rank away. So guys kept coming up to me and saying, "Corporal? What did you do, reclass?" Meaning, did I change jobs. I finally got tired of explaining it and just said, "Yes, I reclassed." It was easier.

By then I was twenty years old and was surrounded by mostly inexperienced eighteen-year-olds. The drill sergeants knew I had rank, and they said if I didn't tell these kids anything, they wouldn't mess with me. I reassured them I was just there to do whatever I was told. And I did.

I had a really smooth time there, just hanging in the background. I did all the push-ups, watched the guys get frustrated and fight each other. You know, all the stuff we did in my first basic training. This time, I was mainly amused by it, since I knew what it was about. It was a joke, really. If it's your first time through, it's not a joke because you don't know what to expect. You think they really *are* going to kill you.

We did a lot of things I hadn't done in my first non-infantry basic training. We did live-fire exercises where you had to crawl under barbed wire and guys would shoot over you. Of course, it's probably five feet above your head and there's barbed wire above you, so you can't stand up even if you wanted to, but it's loud and it's kind of real. We also learned ground-fighting techniques and ways to gain control over a noncombative, which you might encounter in villages— untrained civilians making aggressive moves. It built on what I'd learned as a high-school wrestler. As helpful as that training was, when I got to my first assignment at the 101st, I realized I still did not know *anything*. Basically, I'd been through kindergarten.

And the end of basic training, of course, there was a graduation ceremony. This time my mom, girlfriend, and youngest brother came. That graduation wasn't as meaningful to me as the first, but it was cool having them there.

I returned to South Florida and packed, then shipped off to the 101st around October of 2002. I arrived at Fort Campbell, Kentucky, for in-processing, a holding-pattern environment with barracks. At this point, I had been in the National Guard for three years, technically, because everything had counted since my senior year of high school. So I was signing up for another three to finish out my original contract.

There were women as well as men at the 101st, and we were in similar situations. A lot of them were right out of basic training. But you might have a lieutenant colonel or a sergeant coming from Germany to the 101st, or from Korea. You saw all ranks of officers and enlisted. The first day, they handed me this huge brown envelope, and I went from one building to the next, just following orders. The in-processing was supposed to last a week, and then they would cut our orders. Since I was infantry, I would be assigned to one of the three infantry brigades.

Each brigade has had its big moment in history. The first brigade was known because of the Siege of Bastogne during the Battle of the Bulge. Those were the guys who were surrounded in World War II, and General Patton had to go save them. They were outnumbered five to one. Most of the guys had boots that were not waterproof and stood up to their knees in snow for weeks. The Germans couldn't kill them, couldn't get them to quit. They kept sending them notes like, *Surrender or you're going to die.* The general would write back, *Nuts.* That was his response. They're very proud.

The second brigade was the 502nd. They were real proud as well and had a lot of history in World War II.

The third brigade was the Rakkasans. Loosely translated from Japanese, it means "falling down umbrella men," which is what the soldiers were nicknamed by locals who observed them parachute training during World War II.

Among the newly enlisted, the Rakkasans was the most feared brigade. All over Fort Campbell, I heard people say, "Just pray you don't go to the Rakkasans because all you're going to do is run your ass off. You're going to be in the woods all the time. While you're out in the woods, someone's going to be seducing your wife." This is the kind of stuff people would tell you. Two of the brigades were on one side of the post, but the Rakkasans were all the way on the other side by themselves.

One day, I went over and looked at the Rakkasans' area, and right away I could tell that it had a different feel. The layout was more linear, structured, and it had that huge red Rakkasan torii (Japanese gate) logo everywhere, which told me they had a lot of pride. The guys walked differently, with a purpose, and I could feel the energy. I walked into the headquarters and asked to speak to the sergeant major. The kid at the desk was on CQ duty—Charge of Quarters, basically a twenty-four-hour shift that everybody has to do once a month. You have to sit behind this desk the entire time with no TV, no magazines, and no cell phone. The only thing you're allowed to do is answer the phone, brief people who come in, and look at Army training manuals.

Most of the stuff you already know. It's just the most boring twenty-four hours of your life. I walked in, and this bored kid looked at me and said, "Corporal?"

"Yeah," I said. I didn't bother explaining. "I'd like to see the sergeant major."

Now the sergeant major is the highest guy in the brigade. He's got easily five thousand men under him. This is the highest rank you can be as an enlisted man. Most guys don't make it to brigade sergeant major, especially not in the Rakkasans. So this CQ kid figured I must be confused. "Um, are you lost? I mean, what do you want?"

An E4 like me was not even really allowed to talk to the E9, the sergeant major, but I kept going. "I'm over at processing, and I want to see if the sergeant major will give me a letter of recommendation to be a Rakkasan."

The CQ looked at me and said, "Dude, you need to get the hell out the door. Haven't you heard about the Rakkasans? You don't want to be in this unit. I'm telling you, it sucks." I stood there, studying him for a moment. I kind of felt sorry for him; he didn't belong in a unit this proud.

About that time, another guy walked up. "You want to see the sergeant major?"

I said yes.

He started grinning, like, *I'll go get him, this is going to be funny.*

He walked back with this guy who looked like death. The sergeant major was probably about forty, but he looked ancient. Twenty-something years in the infantry will absolutely crush you. It's like playing linebacker in the NFL for twenty years. You just can't do it.

A lot of what we do in infantry is road marching with a rucksack—we call it "humping." But you can't hump a ruck for twenty years without ruining your knees, hips, ankles, back, and shoulders. Then you've got all the wars you're going to fight in. There are going to be scars. I remember this one sergeant major who had a scar from his forehead to his cheek, right through his eye. The eyeball had a grey slash through it where the color should have been. It was kind of hard to look at. It's really a brutal life.

Anyway, he looked at me and this rough voice rumbled out. "Who are you?"

I answered fast, "I'm Corporal Murphy, Sergeant Major."

"Corporal? How the fuck are you a corporal?" I was thinking, *Oh god, here we go again.* He didn't wait for an answer. "What do you want?"

I told him I was in processing and that I wanted a letter of recommendation to be a Rakkasan.

"Give me your file." I handed it to him. He pulled out my range card, the expert record, then put it back in and nodded. "That's good." He pulled out my Physical Training (PT) score and nodded again. "That's good." He looked at me. "You married?"

I said, "No, Sergeant Major."

And he said, "Good. Because if you were married, I wouldn't take you." Of course, that's not true, they take married guys all the time, but it brought home his point. It was a serious job, and marriage complicates things.

I stood there, realizing that what I had just done was way out of the norm. With processing, you're supposed to just wait your turn; you get an order, and it tells you whatever unit you're going to be in. That's how you find out where you're going. Nobody—nobody—is dumb enough to go sign up to be in the Rakkasans. You're usually assigned, and most guys would not be happy about it.

The sergeant major turned to the CQ kid. "Write him a letter of recommendation." It was done and signed in two minutes: *Sergeant Major Savusa, Rakkasans Command Brigade Sergeant Major, assigns this man to the Rakkasans.*

"Thank you, Sergeant Major!"

I went back to processing and handed them the paper. The guy behind the desk looked stunned. "Are you freaking crazy?"

I said, "No, I just don't like sitting around."

There was some relief to have that part over. I hated the processing part of basic training. I hated not knowing where I was going. I was ready to face anything, if only I could get started. After a few minutes more of disbelieving looks and wisecracks, they cut the orders and handed them to me. "Good luck."

I went to the barracks to get my bags, and all the guys I had been hanging out with the previous few days were saying, "You got orders?"

"Yup."

"How?"

I told them that I had gotten a letter of recommendation from the Rakkasans. They couldn't believe it. *Hadn't I heard?* I said I wasn't worried about the Rakkasans. Maybe it would be the infantry regiment from hell, I didn't know. I would soon find out that it was every bit as hard as everybody had said.

Now loaded down with my stuff, I headed back to the 187th Infantry Regiment. They had three battalions at the time, and I ended up with the Iron Rakkasans, which is the most famous of the battalions, but that was just by chance. I handed them my orders, and the first thing the guy said was, "Corporal? How did you…" And I explained it for the ten thousandth time.

I was assigned to Bravo Company. There's an A, B, C, and D. Bravo Company's nickname and motto is "Battle Hard." In their office, some silly-looking guy was pushing paperwork behind a desk, and he checked off my papers and sang, "Gooood luck." I headed upstairs to the first sergeant's office for my platoon assignment.

I gave three short knocks on the door and heard "Enter." The first sergeant was sitting at his desk as I walked in, and he told me to take a seat. I saw framed photos on the wall of him with all the men he'd been in charge of moving up through the ranks, the tours he'd served, and his accomplishments. He was probably forty with patches from all these schools he'd been in—Airborne, Air Assault, Ranger. I didn't have anything but corporal on *my* uniform, which everybody thought was a joke anyway.

He glimpsed at my paperwork, then looked across his desk without smiling. "You know we're going to war, don't you?"

I said, "I kind of figured, First Sergeant."

He nodded. "Do you have any questions?"

I said, "Well, are we going to do any training before we go?"

"Probably not, there's no time."

All I could think was, *That's not good.* The rest of the guys had just gotten back from Afghanistan. They had been to combat, and here I was a friggin' cherry. Sure, I had some rank, but I had no experience. Even guys with less rank than me had no respect for me. I knew I would be tested until I proved myself.

I told the first sergeant my immediate concern: "I've never been in a helicopter, and we're about to go to Iraq." It hadn't been announced or anything, but Iraq was all over the news. Saddam Hussein was not letting the weapons inspectors in. Bush was warning them, "If you don't let them in, we're going to come over there."

The first sergeant shrugged. "Helicopter? Just think of it as a taxi ride into combat."

I said, "A taxi ride?"

He closed my file, pushed it to the side of his desk, then stood up. "Yeah, some guys go by Bradley Fighting Vehicle (a small tank used for transport), some guys jump in by parachute. This is an Air Assault

Division, so we're going to go in by helicopter. It's just our means of getting there."

I thought, *There's got to be more to it than that.* And I was right—there's a hell of a lot more to it, as I would soon learn on the initial invasion of Iraq.

The meeting, which lasted maybe two minutes, was over. I was officially a Rakkasan.

That first day with my platoon, they gave me the 101st patch. Every time I walked by a mirror, I looked at it. *Finally.* It looked a lot better than that National Guard patch I used to have that nobody recognized. Anybody could recognize the screaming eagle. My platoon sergeant also came up with a solution to the rank of corporal. He decided I was going to be a specialist at E4, so the corporal title went away and I put on the specialist patch. No problem, as it was the same rank. I was just glad I didn't have to explain my status anymore.

Even with the two new insignias, I was still the only guy whose right shoulder was bare, and that was eating at me. When you go into combat in the Army, whatever unit you go with, you wear that patch on your right shoulder for the rest of your career. Every guy there had a patch on both shoulders because they had all been to Afghanistan.

If you go to war as an infantryman, you wear the combat infantryman badge—the CIB—over your left breast pocket. It's a rifle with a wreath around it, and it's a true badge of honor. Every guy that's in the infantry wants one. A lot of guys were in the infantry twenty years in the Clinton and Reagan administrations but were never given the opportunity to earn a CIB. Now, here I was surrounded by CIBs, and some had stars to indicate multiple conflicts. It shows you've used your training. Like a football player who prepares at practice all season and is able to prove himself in the game on Saturday, you want to be a full member of the team, you want to be part of that club. Without a CIB, I felt like a nobody.

Besides all the combat-proven soldiers, there were other things I hadn't seen up to that point. Like snipers walking around in their ghillie suits, camouflage clothing designed to resemble heavy foliage. I thought, *This is the real deal.*

The first sergeant sent me to a squad leader named Hollister. This guy had a mouth full of crooked teeth, and his lip was always full of dip. He wasn't a lean man—in fact, he was kind of on the jolly side—but he was a staff sergeant, and I was a specialist. He had me beat by two ranks. I was respectful and responded to commands promptly: "Yes, Sergeant. No, Sergeant." I did not want to get a bad reputation. I'd learned that lesson from the *Maxim* drill sergeant in Texas.

I definitely was not going to be late or show up in the wrong uniform or fall out of a run or not shoot well. I mean, if you messed up one time in the military, they would remember it for years. *Years.* "Remember that time Murph was late?" You can never be late. In all the years I was in, I was never late once. You can't be. You just can't. It's not a place where people forgive you and then we talk about our feelings.

Hollister told me, "You need to go square away your gear." He was referring to the two duffel bags I had collected back at processing. Things like a canteen, trenching tool (shovel), gas mask, kneepads, and smoke canisters.

I looked at all the stuff and thought, *I don't even know what to do with these things.* Everyone else had already been to war, so they had their gear all settled into their rucksack. Besides the stuff, there were all kinds of directions, like how to attach strips of burlap to your helmet, kind of like Rasta hair, and where to stash your flashlight. You had to follow the company's standard operating procedure, which would be different from company to company. Alpha Company (Angels from

Hell) and Charlie Company (Choppin) did things differently than Bravo Company.

I had guys with less rank giving me the instructions, and all I could say was, "Thank you. Thank you." I was taking notes as fast as I could but was overwhelmed. They said things like, "You've got to take this item to the sew shop where they're going to stitch on this insignia." My unit insignia had to go on this bag and this bag and this bag. Everything was very specific. The scope of the weapon was tied down with a certain type of cord and knot. If it was tied incorrectly, they cut it off and you had to retie it. Your infrared laser had to be tied to your weapon with a different type of knot even though it was also attached by screws. I was trying to learn as fast as I could so I wouldn't make a mistake and never be forgiven.

On the second day, we went to the range and I scored Expert. I thought, *Thank God.* I didn't hit forty out of forty, just thirty-seven out of forty, and at first I was mad, but everyone else was pretty happy with it, so I thought, *Maybe these guys are easy to please.*

Another test was the first run—PT. The other guys in my platoon knew my story because they could see I had rank but didn't have a combat patch or combat extra badge. So they did not respect my rank. They did not respect my previous years because I came from the National Guard, and the regular Army hates the National Guard. They call them the "Nasty Girls." So they were going to try to make me fall out. I could hear it, *Here comes that weekend warrior.* I thought I was never going to get away from that rep.

I found out much later that some of the guys were even little suspicious of me. They thought I might be an investigator with the Criminal Investigation Department—the CID. I spoke differently, didn't have tattoos, and carried myself more like an officer, fueling the rumor. So that was one more strike against me.

As we headed out to do PT, I saw my squad leader, Hollister, whisper something to several of the guys, and I knew they were going to try to run real fast and make me fall out so they could yell at me. Running in formation, a single line, with a squad was kind of new to me. I was used to running in a platoon formation, like I did at basic training, but I managed to stay with them even when they started running faster. Then Hollister screamed, "Murph! Get to the front." I've always had long legs, and I liked the front better anyway because I could actually stretch them out a little bit. If I was in the middle, I had to be careful of every step. I didn't want to hit the guy in front of me, as I knew he might turn around and punch my lights out. Once I got to the front, I just naturally started picking up the pace. I didn't feel it. Until I looked over and saw Hollister just slobbering. I thought, *Aw man, I am about to make* him *quit.* He finally barked, "Slow up!"

After that second day, the rest of the guys backed off a bit. *The guy can shoot and he can run. He'll be fine.*

CHAPTER 9

At the Ready

When you're in the 101st Airborne, you have to always be deployment ready. That means when you get the "go," you grab your bag, grab your weapon, and must be ready to board the aircraft within the hour. With that plan, we can be anywhere in the world in eighteen hours. If the embassy in Benghazi is attacked, they'll send the SEALs or Special Forces immediately. But we'll be sent, too, so your bags are always packed, and your assigned weapons are waiting for you in the vault. If you get an order, you *have* to be there.

But you never know if the call-up is real. Sometimes we'd get called in the middle of the night, load up, board the plane, and take off. Then the pilot would turn the plane around midflight. It was a test.

So you stay on high alert at all times. When the call is real, you're never more ready. You've trained and trained and trained. And you're confident that you're ready to go. Not just you—you're confident in your men, your team, and the gear you have. You cannot go into a fight thinking you're going to lose. You have to believe you are number one. You have to believe that *thoroughly*. It spills over toward arrogance, cockiness—that's just the mentality. But you can't go to war half-cocked. You don't want to shoot any of your own guys or an innocent civilian by doing something that's incorrect. And you could get yourself killed.

That was my biggest fear in active duty—that I might screw up. I would constantly think about all the different ways I could screw up;

I'd go through them all in my head. My next biggest concern when I got into leadership was how to keep everybody else from screwing up.

But for the most part, you get advance notice about deployment. Before my first tour, I had become a team leader, Specialist Murphy, and put in charge of other men. The heat was on. This business is pretty serious, but it gets far more serious just before the date you're deployed. There's this thing called OPSEC, operations security. It means you know something that affects the security of an operation and you're not allowed to talk about it. For example, in 2003, I knew I was going to Iraq, but all I could tell my parents was, *I'm going away for a while*. People are constantly listening to a soldier's conversations, and you could get really hammered for violating OPSEC.

So you see that date, and it's coming, it's coming. You go home one last time and see your mom. She starts crying. You tell your friends and you're hoping they'll lighten up and party with you, but they just don't get it and end up saying all the wrong things. I had some people say things to me like, "I'm sorry you have to go over there and do that," which I guess meant fight for their freedom. If they'd said nothing, it would have been better.

It's like you have to be strong when no one else is—and you're the one who's going to be affected. You've got to be the leader back at the base in Fort Campbell, the strong one back home and with your friends. And with your girlfriend or your wife or kids. All that makes it a lot harder on a soldier. But you've got to man up, do whatever it takes. It makes a guy a little colder. You have to basically be the pillar in every situation the military puts you in and in every relationship back home. It's a sense of responsibility to a mission much bigger than you've ever had before. Your ass belongs to Uncle Sam.

Some people do crazy things like get married right before their deployment, mostly because you can make more money and get more benefits. But some of those guys come home on leave only to find their wife is pregnant with somebody else's kid, they've spent everything and trashed their credit. As if going to war wasn't stressful enough.

Everybody loves their country, but we're fighting for the idea of America, and a lot of people just don't get it. People say, "Thank you for your service," but they don't know the real sacrifice, what kind of impact your choice made on others. I sometimes find myself thinking about that guy who's sitting there on a bag that's packed, and how he's putting his family through such grief. Our choices profoundly affect our families. In fact, it can come across pretty selfish if you think about it.

The day I was leaving for my first tour, I said good-bye to my family at my dad's house. He was in the kitchen, cleaning up and kind of staying in the background. I knew it was killing him. I pulled him aside for some one-on-one time. "Stay low," he told me, "and remember, Murphys always come home."

I wanted to say good-bye to my girlfriend, Kristine, last. She and I had dated since I was sixteen, and I was now twenty-two. We had been together longer than many of my fellow soldiers had been married, which made saying good-bye really painful. As much as I felt called to this new job, I hated making her cry.

Kristine and I walked out into the yard, and after we said everything we could think of, I got in my truck to leave, and she followed in her car behind me, headed home. But I saw her pull over on the side of the road, so I called to check on her, and she was just a mess. I turned around, and when I got out of my truck, she about tackled me. She was sobbing and shaking. At that point, you don't want to go, but there's nothing you can do.

Kristine finally calmed back down, and I told her it would be fine. I knew I had to keep going. I would miss her, but I had a big job to do.

My friend's dad had been a Marine in Vietnam. I found out later that my deployment gave him nightmares. He dreamed he was there fighting with me, and it triggered an episode of post-traumatic stress disorder.

You just never want to be in this position, to put people through that kind of grief. It makes you feel really bad; you're tearing up your mom, your family, your friend's mom. Your girlfriend's crying like a two-year-old—all because of you. Because of your country and the direction they want you to go. That's pretty much what I thought about on my twelve-hour drive back to Fort Campbell.

On some tours, a lot of the guys bring their families back to the base for the good-bye ritual, which I thought had to be even harder. As you're preparing for deployment, the days start to slow down. It's like you're leaving in eight days, then seven, then six. You're getting new equipment, getting a lot of stuff to go over there with.

You finally get down to two days out. In the same company area where you'd meet every morning in shorts and a T-shirt to do push-ups and pull-ups for an hour and a half, you'd start seeing wives coming through, parents, someone's brothers and sisters. In those situations, I couldn't help but think about my own family.

During those final days, you constantly see people hugging and crying. Some of the same soldiers I'd been sweating it out with for hours on end were now holding their newborns. There were little kids running around and teenagers kind of checking it all out. Since I'd said good-bye weeks before, it started to wear on me.

Normally, we'd pick on each other pretty hard, we'd say stuff to humiliate each other. E-mask or unman them. We'd use anything we had on a guy. You might know something about one of the guys, but it would be different when he was there holding his girlfriend. To her, he's Rambo. But we knew the truth. The rules changed slightly; we walked around trying to be nice. Even though these people were family, they were not part of our world.

Family members sometimes know that you're the boss, and you never know how they're going to react. One time, I had a guy's mom grab me with her nails, look me in the eye, and say, "Make sure my boy comes home." You know you don't have any control over it, but it's something that sticks with you. Her son was in the convoy when our vehicle got hit and I lost my leg. Thankfully, he made it home without injury.

A lot of the guys are cigarette smokers, and as deployment gets closer, they turn into chain smokers. You're just training so hard physically and mentally. You've spent a year getting ready, and it's like, "Let's get the time started. Just put me in—now." Since you've been training so hard, you've got a lot of energy. And you're fixing to fly for fourteen hours. Tensions are high and you're trying not to step on the toes of anyone who might outrank you.

The day of departure, we loaded up on these old blue buses for a four-mile drive to the airstrip. It's huge, probably ten times the size of Chicago O'Hare but without the nice terminal. The biggest of the big. That's when time really slows down, and the waiting can be especially nerve-racking. At the big hangar, you wait some more. You are there by five a.m., so you can leave at noon. It's always hurry up and wait.

I've always been the guy who needed only ten minutes to do anything, so that part was excruciating for me. The dudes started wrestling and weapons got knocked over. When I was in charge, I did my best to make sure things didn't get out of hand.

I would walk through the line of my guys and have them check all of their sensitive equipment *one more time*. Everyone lined up, dressed in camo and combat boots answering commands. The checks had become second nature. Something I was constantly doing was touching my weapon.

You have a leader card with all your guys' information on it. So you check their ID card, dog tags, and weapons. You look at the serial number of the weapon and make sure it's the same one on the leader card. You also have them check their night vision and tie-downs. We tie our scopes to our weapons and our night vision. We put the night vision in the pocket of our vest and slip the D-ring onto the vest. You've got to double plan for everything. There's a saying: "One is none, two is one."

Even if you're going on a simple mission, you never know what can happen. Say you're the radio telephone operator (RTO). You have a fresh battery that's going to last four days. Well, you bring an extra one. Batteries weight five pounds and those pounds add up. But you've got to have it.

We've got a lot more gear than normal passengers. We've got two huge duffel bags that are stored underneath the plane. We write our unit name on the bags; that way, when a thousand green bags come out, you know whose is whose. So all the A-Co (Alpha Company) 3-187s go here, all the 2-187s go there. Code markings are done with reflective tape. They look like slashes, similar to a captain rank in the Army. You might have two stripes or three in different color combinations. And we'll also have cat eyes—reflective straps with a shape and color specific to your unit, so you can see your bag at night. These are on our helmets, too, so you know whom you're following in the dark. It helps in identification.

We've also got "handheld" backpacks that aren't as small as they sound. This always includes a woobie, a nylon camouflage poncho liner that doubles as a blanket because we have to sleep wherever the hell we are. We might be sleeping in an airport, we might be sleeping on a tarmac, we might be sleeping in the desert when we get there. And, of course, we have our night vision and our weapons.

On my first day with the Rakkasans, all that stuff I was assembling was called TA-50 gear (Table of Allowances 50), everything a soldier needs in combat. Throughout your training missions, if you lose a canteen or a poncho, it's up to you to go buy it on your own. If you rip it or it's somehow destroyed, the Army will inspect it and throw it in the trash before replacing it, but you have to go through the right channels.

Just before boarding, we got into chalk lines, platoon-sized units. I made sure I had all my guys. I'd ask them something for the third time and they'd answer nervously.

The airline usually tries to make the flight memorable for soldiers. When we boarded the aircraft for my second deployment, there were streamers hanging from the ceiling, all in red, white, and blue. The civilian flight attendants were wearing camouflage aprons. They were decked out and ready to do their part.

Military aircraft are not comfortable for flying. The C-5 Galaxy is one of the largest military aircraft in the world and is mostly used to transport cargo, but it can accommodate about seventy troops. And a C-17 is not very accommodating at all, even though it can haul a seventy-ton M-1 Abrams tank and a hundred troops. But we don't always fly military aircraft. For both of my tours, I was on a regular commercial plane. Some of us are carrying really big weapons, like the M240 bravo, "the pig," or the M249 squad automatic weapon (SAW), "the piglet." Try to picture those on a commercial airline. Some have built-in tripods or legs that stick out, which make them difficult to maneuver on an aircraft. It's not reasonable to think that a guy could fly thirteen hours with a thirty-pound machine gun in his lap, so we stacked them in exit rows. The largest machine guns would be facing each other, and the smaller ones were loaded on top.

It's kind of comical seeing these flight attendants—civilians—stepping over machine guns that are sticking out into the aisle, "Excuse me, excuse me," and hoping they don't topple the pile.

The officers go up front in first class, naturally. We had hundreds of Joes—enlisted guys including squad leaders, team leaders, sergeants, privates—all in the back. There are different routes to the Middle East, but for us it's about an eight-hour flight to Europe—London or Italy—then another four or five to Kuwait or into Iraq directly.

CHAPTER 10

Her Fantasy, My Nightmare

On my first tour, I had a private who was a bit of a problem child. Rousch always seemed to get in trouble for things. He was a good kid, he just wasn't cut out for the infantry. And he was smart, but he couldn't seem to get the simple things right—like arriving on time and wearing the correct uniform.

Right before we boarded the aircraft, Rousch complained about a swollen knee. He had some kind of an infection, and he couldn't bend his leg because of the swelling. This wasn't good. I was the team leader for a three-man team. The truth was, I needed four men, so I was running a little underpowered with only two other guys. And now one of them was looking hurt.

The standards for infantry are very high. An infantry guy's uniform won't always be clean because of the rigors of the job, but his equipment will be immaculate. His physical appearance will be strong, he'll be in good shape, his haircut will be better than anyone else's. Whatever he's got will not just meet the standard but exceed it.

The infantry is the macho-est of the macho. You don't have a sexy job, you don't have a clean job, you don't have an easy job, a cake job. It's a really, really tough job. So at the end of the day, all you've got is bravado. It just supersedes any other job, physically, in the military. That means if you're sick, you've got to suck it up, you've got to come into work. If you're really ill, then we'll send you home to recover. But no matter how bad off you are, you have to at least come in and let your higher-ups see you. We've got to have accountability.

Because we pick on each other so much and jump on any sign of weakness, some of the others were asking, "Hey, what's wrong with your guy? Does he have vaginitis?"

I was doing my best to defend Rousch. "Go look at his leg, it's swollen. He can't bend it. Hopefully we can get it fixed, 'cause we need him." Rousch may not have been my best guy, but he was one of our guys and a crucial member of the firepower. Rousch carried the SAW, the most casualty-producing weapon on the team. I had to have the SAW; I needed that weapon in the fight. I could not maneuver my men and run the big gun at the same time.

So Rousch was sitting in the rear of the plane where he could stretch his leg out. I went back to check on him and found a flight attendant nursing him with this worried look on her face.

That is not the infantry way. We're expected to be macho, even if we're blown up. And here's Rousch, just looking pitiful. He had this little washcloth on his forehead. And now this flight attendant who was coddling him gave me a look like, *Who are you?* I felt like saying, *Get off my guy. Stop pampering him. We've got drugs, we'll cut on him if we need to, but this motherly stuff has got to go.*

I held my tongue and said, "Hey, Rousch, how are you doing?"

He said, "Specialist Murphy, I'm not doing so good. It's getting worse, it hurts more." So I started touching around the knee to get an idea of the size it was before, and he winced. I took a marker out, drew a ring around the red part as a baseline so I could check it hours later and see if the infection had spread.

Out of the corner of my eye, I saw this flight attendant's face get that softy look like, *Aw, you're so nice, you're so cute.* I had just turned twenty-two, but I was a team leader. I was in charge, and I was just doing my job. I felt like saying, *Are you serious?* I was doing my best to stay focused, in the zone. I knew this plane was going to the Middle East, and I didn't know what we were flying into. There was this cloud above us and it was war—that's about all I knew. Still, I tried to be nice and remember my southern manners, even calling her ma'am.

I came back a few more times to check on Rousch, stepping over the various weapons sticking out into the aisles, and the flight attendant made sure she was there. She also came by my seat when she was serving the soldiers drinks, adding to the already crowded feeling. Her hair was pulled back tight from her round face; she wore a blue neck scarf and was all cheeks. She probably had ten years on me. Still, she gave me that nervous smile, the flirty thing that teenage girls do. All I could think was, *Are you serious? I don't know what you're thinking, but I don't want to know, either.*

We finally landed in Kuwait, and all the men gathered their gear, preparing to leave. That flight attendant cornered me near the front before I could deplane and said, "I don't want you to go." I gave her this incredulous look, like, *Who the hell are you?* I already had to say good-bye to my family and my girlfriend; that was hard enough. But this lady? I didn't even know her!

I finally answered, "I don't know what you're talking about," and she said, "You know there are places on board I could hide you." Omigosh, she was serious! She kept going, "You're so nice, and look what you did for your guy."

I said, "Lady, that's my job." Some of the guys overheard this exchange and, of course, they started making fun of me. I told them, "Knock it off, or I'm gonna beat the hell out of you." I turned around, and that lady grabbed me by the lapel of my shirt and kissed me. Right on the lips.

I pulled away and turned to head off the plane. The guys who'd seen the kiss said, "What was all that about?" I just shook my head. "I. Don't. Know." Of course, they didn't believe me.

I was still frustrated about Rousch, really worried that my three-man team—which was already too small—had just become a two-man team. With three, at least you could spend a third of your time helping to carry the load and alternating night watch schedules, but it was looking like it would be more like fifty-fifty. I wasn't even sure how I was going to get Rousch and his gear off the aircraft.

Before it was over, Rousch would be sidelined with the knee problem and sent to a different unit. He did not participate in the invasion. And I went to war with just one other guy. It was a nightmare.

CHAPTER 11
Tip of the Spear

When you fly into combat, everybody has way more stuff than they need. After you arrive, you slowly start chucking a little bit here and there, or you find another way to compartmentalize, or you might get left in one spot for a while, and maybe you find a cardboard box and use it as a shelf. Guys start becoming expedient.

But when you first go over, you look like a gypsy bandwagon. The infantry guys aren't quite as bad. Of all the military occupational specialties, we are the most squared away—we have to be, because we're carrying everything on our backs. We don't have trucks to haul all our belongings. But you've still got too much crap. You've got a bulging rucksack on your back. Then you've got an assault pack, also on your back, and a small backpack that comes with the rucksack, which you strap to your chest. That's three bags. Then you've got an A-bag, a long duffel stuffed with essentials issued by the Army. You're wearing a vest with thirty pounds of body armor, your weapon clipped to your shoulder, and a helmet, and you're usually carrying additional bags in each hand. So you look a little ridiculous walking around.

When you first arrive, your uniform is brand new, too, so you look different than everybody else because they've been in theater for a few months. Their stuff is faded from the sun, from being washed in a bucket, and it's filthy from work. Here you show up with this clean pack and clothing and you look like a day-one freshman in college. You're an easy mark, and everyone takes advantage of it. When you're a private, you're a cherry. Even up to one year in combat, you're a cherry. The Marines call those on their first ride "boot"—like, "You dumb boot." For us, it was "cherry," as in, "Shut up, cherry, get outta here." You graduate from cherry to being just a Joe. A Joe is not a leader, but they're part of the team.

As much as I hated sitting around waiting to receive orders when I was stateside, it was even worse with deployment. You're ready to just get it over with, to get it started. There was a lot of waiting to get shipped to the Middle East, then once in Kuwait, you're waiting for the action to start.

We arrived in Kuwait in February of 2003 for the initial invasion. The Army kept us occupied initially with all-day training and alternating night guard shifts. When you're not on a particular mission, the Army keeps everyone busy so they don't have a lot of time to think. Thinking could lead to "I don't want to be here"; it can lead to negativity. And one bad apple can affect the morale of a lot of people.

There's no such thing as a routine in theater. Even if you received a briefing one day about the next day's events, and you spent the day preparing, everything they told you would change by that evening. And change again before the next day. Leadership never leaves time for you to micromanage your own time; they keep you in a state of not knowing. It's designed to keep you on your toes, keep you tough, to help you avoid complacency. They tell you when it's time for personal hygiene in the morning and how much time is allowed. That training will help you survive. If you find yourself in a terrible battle for weeks, you know what it means to be in constant state of alertness.

At the forward operating base, we might get one hot meal a day trucked in, but there were days and weeks when we lived on MREs (Meals Ready to Eat). They throw out boxes of MREs and you grab one. No cherry picking—whatever your hand lands on is what you eat. You might get chicken tetrazzini or meatloaf for breakfast three days in a row.

As much as the Army tries to manage morale, they did a terrible job of managing our expectations in Iraq, preparing us mentally. They told guys that they'd probably be home to see their kids in a few months, before summer. Nobody thought it would be a year. Think about it: if I tell you I'm going to hold you underwater for ten seconds and you've got to be able to do it, and then I hold you under for fifty seconds, you're not going to be happy. It just made the mission more difficult.

* * *

Our division commander, Major General David Petraeus, told our battalion that we would have a special role once we got to Iraq. We had no idea what that meant, but we assumed we'd get there like everybody else, going in on what was called the GAC, Ground Assault Convoy.

For weeks, we laid out our gear, and they worked out some big order of movement—where your truck would be. They had constant meetings. Finally, they lined up all the vehicles for the GAC. But at the last minute, they decided to jump our battalion in by helicopter. That "special role" meant we were being sent to the front first. The tip of the spear. It ended up being the longest air assault in history. We flew hundreds of miles past the Iraq-Kuwait border, through the Scud missile sites, through little towns and the desert, and we were dropped in without any kind of support besides air support—and that's if we could get it. The rest of the Army came in on the GAC.

It was my first time in a helicopter. In training, we practiced how to get on and off when it landed, how to do a half moon when you get out to protect the bird, what happens if you land on an incline and how to avoid the tail. And I knew that the rotors created a huge amount of wind, and with your rucksack, it could knock you over. But I still didn't know *anything*.

We flew over the convoy, and it was incredible to see thousands of tanks, trucks, and other vehicles in formation for miles on end. Some of the vehicles were desert tan, while others were Army green, but each had an orange three-foot marking on top so they could easily be recognized as an American military vehicle. As we approached our drop-off point, the helicopter pilot radioed back, "Five minutes." The leader with the headset yelled, "Five minutes," and it was repeated loudly—"Five minutes!"—down the line so everyone could hear it over the roar of the helicopter. Then it was, "One minute...one minute...one minute."

When we finally hit the ground, it was not one of those Hollywood soft landings. We slammed down so hard, I thought we had crashed. The pilot wanted us out of the aircraft as quickly as possible since he was a fairly large target and extremely vulnerable when not moving. But we were so cramped in those helicopters our legs didn't work. As each of us rolled out of the bird, it took a couple guys to help another one up because our rucks were two hundred pounds. Beyond my standard infantry load, I was also carrying mortar rounds for the mortar section and extra radio batteries for the RTOs. They had divided equipment that far down. I had never, honestly, held a mortar round before. Soldiers with mortars usually carry their own tubes along with the base plate for mounting the tube. But since we didn't know what to expect or how long we'd be in combat—maybe a month, two months, three months—things got spread all the way down to where it was, "Hey, Murph, here's a mortar round. Why don't you put that in your bag?" It was an order, so I didn't get a choice. I had everything but the kitchen sink, and now all of a sudden here comes the kitchen sink.

One of our first missions was to guard a forward arming and refueling point they called FARP Shell. Imagine a giant bladder lying in the desert with cords coming out of each corner. That's a blivet, or a portable storage tank that held hundreds of gallons of fuel. Our helicopters would drop down, hook up, and refuel. They put our company in a defensive position, a series of shallow foxholes about three hundred yards apart and in the shape of a big *L*, to guard the fuel. We stayed in a fighting position 24/7. Sleep was by rotation, and since it was just me and one other guy on my team, one of us always had to be awake. There was no such thing as good rest; you were doing well to get twenty minutes at a time.

A day or two into it, the radio alerted us that there was a white truck trying to enter our perimeter. It drove toward us, then saw the guys and backed up. Then it drove a perpendicular mile and tried to do the same thing again. To me, it looked like the truck was trying to get around us. Someone called in that they were trying to probe us, so a Kiowa came in—a helicopter—and decided to shoot it. We later learned it had been a father and a mother and a kid. They killed them all. The military couldn't take any chances, you know. I saw the truck but was not ordered to shoot it, so I wasn't directly affected. But it was pretty sad.

We waited there about five days, living in the wide-open desert, when we were hit with the sandstorm from hell. Even the Iraqis said it was the worst they'd seen in twenty years. Some of the enemies believed it was Allah helping them, because it grounded all our birds and left guys like me out there in the desert with no help, no support.

I was looking out my foxhole about midafternoon and saw this big brown cloud coming. It seemed to be moving about fifty miles an hour toward us. I had never seen anything like it. In my mind, I thought they had dropped a nuke on us or we had detonated a nuclear bomb. The way the dust was rolling in on us was just incredible.

Everybody started yelling, "Get down! Get ready! Get covered up!" Of course, I'd never been to Afghanistan, where they also have dust storms. I'd never been anywhere to experience anything like it. And we weren't sure it was a dust storm. We just knew it looked like hell and it was coming our way.

I was already lying in my hole, which was about two feet deep. We were always down during the day, anyway. We could only stand up at night. We didn't want to give ourselves away out in the middle of the desert. We didn't have a lot of firepower to ward off a big attack. We had javelin rounds so we could take out tanks if needed. And we had radios to call and ask for help. But if a little tank division had been able to get to us while our helicopters and birds were grounded, I don't know if we would have had enough anti-tank rounds to really hold them off for that long. So as a precaution we stayed very close to the ground during the day. We'd stand up and stretch out at night. There was no cigarette smoking at night, either. You couldn't risk somebody seeing the cherry on the end. There was no cigarette smoking in general on most missions, because you could smell it for miles and it might give away your position.

So this sandstorm was coming, and I had no overhead cover. I was lying in my hole, and I looked at the guy to my right. "You ready?" He said, "Yeah, I guess." All of a sudden, it started getting a little dark, like it was five p.m. Then it was as dark as maybe seven thirty, eight p.m. Then it went totally black. I couldn't see my hand in front of my face. And the wind was blowing, peppering me with sand. I had my goggles on, but they weren't enough. The sand was somehow finding a way in, so I closed my eyes. I stayed down with my weapon right under my chest. Then it started raining. Raindrops were pelting us so hard, and my hole started filling up with water. Next it began hailing and my hole filled with of ice. Then came an electric current running sideways through the clouds, everywhere. It was unbelievable. In my mind, there was no way this was a sandstorm. This was a nuclear bomb or something. Lightning going sideways through the clouds was the only thing I could see, otherwise it was solid black. Finally, the wind started to ease up and light slowly returned—back to eight thirty p.m., then seven thirty, six, and five thirty. It never completely cleared up that day before evening came. And by dark my hole was filled with mud from all the ice melting. Unfortunately, I didn't know that mud had been running down the front of the hole and down between my chest and my weapon. It had gone down the barrel of my rifle and all the way down into the bolt, which is the operating system to make the weapon shoot semi-automatic.

So when I was sure the storm was over, I dropped my magazine and could see that my weapon was dirtier than hell. I tried to pull back the action with the charging handle, but it wouldn't move. It was totally clogged, like it had been filled in with concrete. I dropped all the components of the rifle right there in the desert, and I told the soldier next to me I had to take my weapon apart. I cleaned and I cleaned and I cleaned, but it still would not work. There are special solvents and brushes for problems like this, but in the desert I had only a basic gun-cleaning kit. I worked on it for more than an hour and finally got that thing working. But I still didn't trust it, I wasn't confident it would fire, and that's a vulnerable feeling.

CHAPTER 12

Hanging from the Hood of a Humvee

One of the guys who was fairly new to our battalion was Sergeant Troy Jenkins from Alabama. He had been in the Marine Corps for four years and got out. Like a lot of these guys, he wanted to get back in, but it's really hard to get back into the Marines, so he joined the Army. I hate to say that, but yeah, Army was his second choice. And he made his mark. He was with the Rakkasans during Operation Anaconda in 2002, which was the largest firefight at that time, and was eventually transferred to my battalion.

I knew that Jenkins had been a Marine and was a tough guy. He had proven himself in Afghanistan, and I was glad to have him. Little did I know he was going to save my life.

We were finally done with the fuel tank assignment and moved on to our primary mission with the Third Infantry Division: the initial assault on Baghdad. We were right at the front and headed toward what was then the Saddam Hussein International Airport. Estimates of the strength—how many insurgents would be there waiting for us— were astronomical. It was way more than I thought they would send an element our size to fight. We generally like to work with three-to-one odds if we can: three of us against every bad guy. If you look back in history, if you've got a hundred Americans who know the land, and if they're in decent shape, not shot to hell or too hungry, and if they've got enough bullets, a hundred Americans could easily kill three hundred bad guys anywhere in the world. We're just way better. But that's not how we fight. We like to fight three to one, and if we don't have that advantage, we can always call in some other asset and help bring it down to where we have better odds.

So they told us there would be thousands in the opposition, but what they didn't tell us was that the Air Force had been bombing them relentlessly for a week, which had knocked down the numbers considerably.

It was our turn to get into the trucks the Third Infantry Division was bringing forward in the convoy, which came by FARP Shell and collected us from the foxholes. Another guy and I climbed into this big old LMTV (light medium tactical vehicle) truck, which is used for carrying troops or cargo. It's flat in the front and real high off the ground. When I got in, I saw a guy sitting all alone near the cab of the truck. I looked through his goggles and realized he was black, but you couldn't tell at first because he was completely white from all the dust. We thought we had it bad lying in a sand hole for the last four or five days, but these guys were riding in formation in the desert. If you've ever driven down a dirt road behind another vehicle, you know how dust can fly. So now imagine what it would be like driving behind two or three thousand tanks.

The first thing I noticed was that he looked scared. I said, "What's wrong? Where's your weapon?"

He said something like, "They killed them. They cut their heads off."

I said, "Who? Who did what? What are you talking about?" I didn't get much out of him but read later on that some Iraqis ran out in front of our military trucks on the initial convoy and pretended to be friendly. As soon as the trucks stopped, the Iraqis opened the doors and shot everybody. This man had probably seen the results of the ambush, the bodies of some of our men lying there, so he was totally rattled. I asked again, "Where's your weapon?" He started digging through all this cargo, and I noticed how he was dressed, how he moved, and it was clear he was not infantry. He may have been a cook or a mechanic.

He finally showed me his weapon; it was wrapped in a bag so it wouldn't get any dirtier than it was. It was an M16. Mine was an M4 carbine, smaller than his, but it's the same weapon. It's just shorter and sexier and it's got all these toys on it—an infrared laser and a scope, a surefire tactical light, and all kinds of cool things to help me do my job. Him, he just needed a weapon. The M16 doesn't have anything on it and is way longer than it needs to be, which makes it awkward for clearing corners in a house or just carrying it day to day.

I said, "Get your weapon out of the bag. Get your ass up and put the barrel over the side." I don't remember what his rank was, but I didn't care. He was not acting properly, and he needed to be straightened out. So he did everything I said and seemed glad that we were there and we were going to protect him. I knew that if we got into a firefight I shouldn't expect any help from him. In fact, I'd need to make sure his barrel was pointing in the right direction, or one of us might get shot in the rear.

We took off down the road to pick up the other guys. By the time we left FARP Shell, there were about twenty-five of us in the back of the truck. Orders were being passed down, but everything kept getting changed. They would say, "All right, we're going to go to this location and this is the grid, and you need to memorize it. You can't write it down in case you get captured." By the time we had everything memorized, there was a new order. And within two minutes of that order, there was probably a new order, and they just didn't tell anybody. So we continued to prepare for whatever we were told.

The Rangers were supposed to jump into Saddam Hussein International and secure the airfield. That's a typical Ranger mission. All of a sudden they weren't going to do that. It was going to be the

Eighty-Second Airborne. The Eighty-Second had a day to plan for this, so they were jumping through hoops, trying to figure out who was going to do what. Then at the last minute, "Eh," they said, "the 101st will do it." That's us—the Third Battalion with the Third Infantry Division now riding in the back of these trucks. So we literally had five minutes to prepare. Not acceptable, but that's the speed at which things were advancing. That's how quickly things change on the battlefield.

They decided to let the trucks carrying the 101st move toward the front so we would be in a good position to offload, clear the airport terminal and the area. All of us were crammed into the bed of the truck. We had been driving all day and all night, probably twenty-something hours, and I hadn't gone to the bathroom. I had to go bad. Just before we arrived, they stopped the convoy and let everybody get out, stretch our legs, whatever, before we went in.

We got back into the trucks and were driving down this major highway. We came up on an LMTV like the one we were riding in, and it was burning, smoking, and I thought, *Oh my god, those guys must all be dead.* But I hadn't heard of anyone getting hurt ahead of us, so I was going through other possibilities. As we drove past, the enemy just lit into us; they opened up on us with automatic machine guns from the side of the road. It didn't sound like AK-47s. It sounded belt fed, maybe their version of our M60 machine gun (like Rambo had).

My first firefight. Everything just seemed to slow down, it was very, very loud, and I thought it sounded like a concert but a lot louder. You know how when your ears hit that decibel that's a little uncomfortable? It was way louder than I thought it would be, bullets were ripping over our heads, coming from the opposite side of the truck from where I was sitting. I felt the brakes on our vehicle trying to bring the giant tires to a halt. We were very heavy, and it takes a lot to slow one of these trucks down. I started to move, because the last order I'd heard was that if the vehicles stopped and we were under fire, we were to get out. The words they used were "un-ass the vehicle." Get the hell out. Then once you're out, hit the ground and shoot back. Then listen to your leaders, because they're probably going to put you in a squad attack that would take you right to the shooters and eliminate them.

It was my job to open the tailgate. I had practiced it. I had to take the little latch, pull it up, and then slide it to the left, and then push it, jiggle it, and it would open. I had been practicing it over and over. I had my weapon in my right hand, and it was attached at the butt to my right shoulder. Each of us had a male-end clip on our shoulder and a female clip tied to the rifle. That way if you needed both hands you could just let the weapon go and it would slap up against your body. I was holding the pistol grip with my right hand while my left hand was working the lock. The world seemed to be moving in slow motion, like when you're first waking up in the morning. Bullets were cracking, and I could see confusion in people's faces. Our guys on the other side of the truck were shooting back.

The vehicle finally stopped, and I opened my side of the tailgate and looked to the other side. The guy over there hadn't unlatched his side. I thought, *Hell with him. I did my side. I'm getting out of this thing.* I figured if need be, I would hit the ground, run over to his side, and unlatch it for him. But as soon as I stood up to jump, the truck lunged forward and spun me into a full frontal flip out of the back of the vehicle. I fell seven feet to the ground and landed on my head.

I was dazed at first, and then I thought, *Oh, shit.* My weapon had been torn off my body in the fall. I had been holding the pistol grip with my right hand, but the end of my rifle, which was attached to me, got caught on something, and I could see it up in the truck still stuck to whatever had caught the monkey grip. I thought, *Oh, this is not happening!* The truck was moving, so I ran to catch up and grabbed onto the tailgate. There was nothing to put my foot on, no bumper, hitch or anything. My arms were straight up in the air as I held on. If it had been chest high, I could have just jumped in quickly. But there was no way to swing my legs up at that height, and the truck was rolling faster and faster.

My feet were dragging on the ground and burning. I was screaming, "Guys! Guys!" but the insurgents were still shooting and our men were firing back, so nobody would pull me in. My side of the truck wasn't taking fire, but they had to remain focused in case it was a double ambush. They weren't shooting; they were just scanning the highway and staying low. And there I am dragging behind the truck.

Eventually, I couldn't hold on any longer and let go. My boots were on fire from dragging. I rolled about twelve times, which was painful. When I came to a stop, I felt dirt and rocks hitting me, and I realized that the ambushers had fixed their aim on me now.

There I was on the ground with no rifle to shoot back. I was pissed off. I couldn't believe this had happened. I briefly remembered a song that a drill sergeant sang in boot camp: "One day you'll be alone, all alone in the combat zone." My face was in the dirt as low as it could get. My arms and legs were spread and I was trying to see where the shots were coming from, but it was probably four hundred meters. They were just pumping into me and the ground was chipping away. I looked back behind me to see if I could crawl backward and get away from it. I saw a two-strip metal barrier to keep cars on the road, but it didn't offer protection. There was nowhere to go, so I just stayed where I was.

I heard another truck coming. It was part of our convoy. I could see the look on the driver's face: he was hunkered down and gritting his teeth, just trying to get through this ambush. I saw one of our guys on the top of the vehicle with a 240 belt-fed machine gun just hammering away. It looked like Erik Roberts. He was really pumping some rounds. I jumped up and waved my arms, but they blew right past me. Didn't even see me. I dove to the ground again and the fire returned. They were still trying to kill me.

I heard another truck and ran out in front of it, hoping they wouldn't hit me. I saw the guy in the passenger seat point at me and could see him yelling, "Stop! Stop!" The driver's face told me he didn't want to stop, not in a damn ambush. I recognized him as a guy who had started with the infantry but decided he didn't want to fight anymore. He was a conscientious objector. He wasn't allowed to be in an infantry platoon and was sent to headquarters to drive trucks and be a POAG. Of all the people I had to rely on to save my ass! I recognized the guy beside him, Sergeant Troy Jenkins. I ran to the window, and Jenkins yelled, "Get in!" I headed to the back of the vehicle and realized it was all tied down—the cargo was secured by hundreds of cords. I tried to get through the rib but knew it was going to take an hour. Jenkins screamed, "Get on the front!" So I ran and dove onto the hood of the Humvee.

Now every Humvee in the 101st Airborne division has these hooks on the hood and rear, because we're an air assault division now and the vehicles might need to be sling-loaded and transported by helicopter. But somehow I managed to jump on the only Humvee in the 101st without those dang hooks, so all I had to hold onto were the windshield wipers. We were still being sprayed with hundreds of rounds as the vehicle pulled away. I could see Jenkins's face and the driver. They were scared, but probably not as scared as me on the hood of that truck.

My head was facing the passenger's side, and my feet were facing the driver's side, and I was clinging hard to those windshield wipers. The insurgents continued to shoot. As we picked up speed, I realized they had fired an RPG at us—a rocket-propelled grenade. It was coming right for us. It sounded like a huge bottle rocket, and I thought, *This is it.* The driver and Jenkins were still wincing from all the bullets pinging off the vehicle; they had no idea an RPG was on its way. The Hummer was roaring, we were doing about thirty miles per hour, but it was too slow. RPGs aren't the fastest things; they're not like a regular bullet. There's usually just enough time to see it and go, *Oh shit.* Most guys don't see them coming, but I was facing that direction, and it was all I had to look at. Well, that RPG hit a dirt mound, then scurried off into the air and exploded. It didn't hit anywhere near us. I couldn't believe it. I mean, it was perfectly tracked until it hit something, or maybe it just went wild. I don't know.

The Humvee finally got up to about sixty miles an hour, and I was on the hood still hanging on for dear life. I just knew I was going to get my ass chewed when I got back, even though I was following the orders I'd gotten: get out of the truck, un-ass the vehicle.

We finally caught up to the rest of the vehicles. They had taken a right turn just before the airport, down a dirt road with heavy, big walls on either side. I remember thinking this was a terrible road to be on because ten feet to the left was a wall and ten feet to the right was a wall. It would be a perfect choke point for an ambush. Nobody tried, though, and I remember being so glad I'd gone to the bathroom before experiencing my first firefight.

When the convoy stopped, I got off the hood and thanked Jenkins and the driver. I needed to get back to my platoon, so I ran up to the other Hummer. One of my buddies said, "Are you all right, man?" They handed me my M4 and I snatched it, "Yeah. Thanks. I was trying to get back on the truck, and nobody would pull me in."

They said, "Sorry, man. Things got a little crazy."

My squad leader went up to the first sergeant and said, "Hey, we've got Murphy back."

The first sergeant looked puzzled. "Back? When was he missing?"

"When the vehicles stopped, he dropped his side tailgate and jumped out," my squad leader explained.

The first sergeant was livid: "We weren't supposed to get out. We were supposed to drive through the ambush. I told everybody that." Well, not *everybody*. He told the leaders that, who were supposed to tell the under-leaders, who were supposed to get it to the squad leaders, who were supposed to get it to the team leaders, which was me. It never got to me.

The first sergeant yelled for me, and I ran up to him. "Yes, First Sergeant?"

"What the hell happened?"

I stood at parade rest, hands behind my back. "Well, First Sergeant, last I heard, if we got hit and the vehicles stopped, we were going to un-ass the vehicle."

My squad leader, who was standing to the side between me and the first sergeant looked at me briefly, then toward the first sergeant defensively. "We didn't say that. We said we were going to blow through the ambush."

I looked at him like, *You aren't doing this right now, are you?* But I knew what I needed to do, which was take it. I couldn't believe it. I almost got killed, and now my integrity and my leadership were being challenged, and I had to suck it up and take it; jump on the grenade.

The first sergeant paused, then looked back at me. "It doesn't matter now, god dammit. Glad you're all right. Come see me later." He turned to walk away, on to the next urgent matter. I was off the hook, for a while at least. I got back to my platoon, and everybody was laughing and slapping me on the back and howling. I guess they thought they'd never see me again. My squad leader was furious because he did not want to be known for having the guy who would go off on his own like that, as if I had done it on purpose.

All I could think was, *Man, this is not how I envisioned war.* Me, all alone out there, not doing so well. Then owing my life to these other soldiers. It's just not how I pictured things. You see the movies. It's not how I thought it would go.

CHAPTER 13

Like a Good Marine

We ended up going into this outer area of the airport where there were some hangars. The American forces, our Third Infantry Division, were hammering the insurgents outside the airport. But the Iraqis had dug in and had fighting positions everywhere. The Air Force had been bombing them, and we were watching it unfold. The Iraqis were shooting artillery but not at the same rate we were. For every three rounds we dropped on these guys, they might shoot one back. Once in a while, above me, in this little compound I was sitting in, waiting to assault the airport, I would hear a bomb dropping—*boom*—and then *tink, tink, tink*, like our building was being hit by return fire. I thought, *Man, somebody needs to kill those guys before they get lucky, you know?*

* * *

About eight weeks after my wild ride on the Humvee, on Saturday, April 19, 2003, we were doing daily patrols in the city. There are a few million people living in Baghdad and hundreds of thousands of visitors coming in daily. The area we were patrolling had three and four-story block buildings on both sides of the street. It was a fairly busy marketplace, mostly a walking village. There weren't many cars on the street where we were patrolling.

With a squad of about ten, I was on the right side of the road, and that same Sergeant Jenkins who saved my life was on the left side. We could see a couple of troops in the front and a couple of troops in the back, so we were about in the center. In the infantry you know every single guy. You know how they walk, you know how they talk, you know where they're from, you know where they keep their letters from home and how many times they read them when they arrive. You know everything. I mean, even if you see them in night vision, you'll know this one's bowlegged and that guy has a little swag when he moves; you'll know who it is. All that knowledge helps when you're patrolling the streets like we were that day.

As we moved through Baghdad, it was like the circus had come to town. The kids had never seen anything like us and gathered to watch like at a parade. As much as we wanted to keep them away, in case something happened, there was nothing we could do. There were thousands of them. I saw some of the local civilians beating children, trying to keep them back. But they were excited and kept running through us, almost swarming.

We had been on our feet the whole day, walking probably ten miles: take a left at this block, a right at that block. My back hurt, my legs hurt. I started thinking about how we were going to get out of the city. How far had we gone, anyway? We would obviously have to go back that same distance.

We were approaching this intersection and a gentleman, an Iraqi, came up to me, trying to tell me something. I said, "Hey, I'm not in charge. Go talk to someone else." So he went over to the interpreter, and I heard them talking to the squad leader in English. I scanned my area as I listened, because that's about the only way you could ever know what's going on. I heard the translator relaying the Iraqi's message: "You're not welcome here. Don't come here." He was trying to drive us away from that part of town. Of course, we were not going to turn around and go away. That's not how it works. I remained alert; things just didn't feel right.

My head was on a swivel, as I scanned windows and rooftops, and suddenly I heard an explosion about eight feet away on Jenkins's side of the road. I remember kind of waking up dazed, like after being knocked out, but I was still on my feet, wobbly. I looked down and saw fragments of flesh and blood on me. I was still trying to understand what had happened when I finally recovered enough to realize I needed to take cover. I had to pull security until I figured out what was going on. As I turned to run, these zip ties on my body armor, used to take prisoners, caught on a roadside stand, and I thought someone had a hold of me—I was so out of it—and I just started striking this thing with my weapon. I demolished that wooden stand before I figured out the only thing holding me back were the zip ties.

I took a knee on this little piece of Bermuda grass. It's so weird the things you think of in combat, but I remember thinking how beautiful it was to have this little piece of grass I could take a knee on rather than concrete or rocks. I looked back at the road and saw half of our squad lying there. In that brief moment, we had just gone down to about fifty percent in firepower. The civilians were screaming and running in all different directions. It was chaos. That was when my training kicked in. Stay calm, stay focused. I knew the steps: secure the perimeter, treat the wounded and call medevac, then get the hell out of there.

I didn't know it at the time, but a little girl had walked up to Jenkins with an explosive. There are different versions of the story, because there were no eyewitnesses, but the one I've heard most is that the seven-year-old tried to hand the explosive to him. She dropped it and he made a split-second decision: he threw his body on it, like a good Marine would do.

But at this point, I didn't know what had happened. I just saw Jenkins lying there; he was paper white because of the massive blood loss. He was conscious and in a lot of pain and had a look of confusion. He was reaching up in the air, and I could see he was missing a few of his fingers. Another soldier and our medic, Pete Tenario, were beside him. Everything seemed to be moving in slow motion. This was one of the biggest, strongest guys in our company, a guy everybody respected, and now he was lying there, hurt. There was nothing I could do. It was up to me to pull security on this huge area.

I looked back and saw one of our other men, a guy from Puerto Rico. He had taken a piece of shrapnel in the mouth and it had broken his teeth and lodged under his tongue. He was bleeding all down the front of his body. I yelled, "Are you all right?" He said, "I'm fine. I think I just bit my lip." It was clear to me that it was way worse than that, but the adrenaline made him feel like he was okay.

In front of him was another young man who had been clipped in the legs. I saw our radio operator, Specialist Day, had been hit in the calf. He was on the ground, grimacing in pain, but I heard him calling in the details of the incident, calmly and even toned as if nothing unusual had happened. Despite being wounded, those who could were still doing their jobs.

I kept thinking, *How the heck are we going to get out of here?* We had no vehicles. I was exhausted, but even if I wasn't, there was no way I could carry even one of the guys ten miles back to the foward operating base. The plan for evacuation wasn't up to me, anyway. I wasn't in charge. There was a squad leader and an E6 who was about to be a platoon sergeant who would call the shots. But it didn't stop me from thinking through the steps.

Specialist Day called for the medevac but was told they didn't want to send a helicopter since we were in the middle of the city and they didn't know if it was a hot landing zone ("hot" meaning it would be under fire). We didn't need another Black Hawk Down, so they sent Humvees instead.

The explosive had taken a piece of meat out of Jenkins's hip; there was no way to tourniquet it. Doc Tenario was very focused, working so feverishly to save Jenkins's life. He pulled a strap off a truck and tied it in a way that put pressure on the wound. Anything to try to stop the bleeding.

I looked over and saw a huge Iraqi man run up and grab the little girl; her dress was draped across his arms. A staff sergeant started yelling at him to bring her back; he wanted to make sure she got evacuated and treated, too. But the Iraqi man probably didn't understand English. We were later told that she died en route to the Iraqi hospital.

When the Humvees arrived forty-five minutes later, another squad came over to secure the perimeter while we loaded the four wounded. We sped through the city, hopping medians and hitting curbs so hard I nearly launched off the top of the vehicle. We got the wounded to the forward operating base, where a chopper could land. The bird took Jenkins to Baghdad ER first, then to Landstuhl Medical in Germany.

I went back to the cramped area where I kept my bedroll and tried to decompress. There were two letters from home—a rarity—and I read them trying not to think about what had just happened.

Later, the Iraqis tried to make us look bad by saying Jenkins was wearing a grenade and that the little girl had innocently pulled the pin. But I'm sure it wasn't one of our grenades. Two or three days before the blast, the Army had collected them, because President George W. Bush had declared that we'd won, the war was over. So it wasn't a grenade, but she handed him something, I am positive of that, and it was an explosive.

There was also a question over whether an Iraqi put the girl up to it with the intention of blowing us up. That's a possibility, as there have been other cases where children were used that way. And I felt the tension after hearing that Iraqi tell our team leader through the interpreter that we were not welcome.

The investigation later concluded, based on the ground marks, that the explosion was not intentional and that the little girl had probably handed him an unexploded submunition of a cluster bomb. Because none of us saw it—we were too busy doing our jobs, flushing the enemy out of the city—we'll never know for sure what happened or how it happened.

Five days later, on April 24, Jenkins died at Landstuhl Regional Medical in Germany. It was tough. He was gone. He was a very important part of us. He was probably the strongest guy in the company, and now he was gone. It was time to move on, even though we mourned heavily. Guys who were the closest to him took it the worst. But it was just something we were going to have to live with, to deal with, so we did.

I found out later that Sergeant Troy David Jenkins was posthumously awarded the Bronze Star, the soldier's medal for heroism; and the Purple Heart. Our medic, Pete Tenario, received a Bronze Star for his role that day in Baghdad, and he deserved it. I saw him work.

The rest of my first tour was full of similar situations. Firefights, ambushes. Sometimes innocent people got killed. Sometimes our boys got hurt. I can see every one of their faces. I can remember how it smelled, I know how the temperature felt and can still hear that weird call to prayer that blasted over the loudspeakers of the mosques throughout the day.

I remember too much.

Finally, in February 2004 it was time to go home. They flew us into Fort Campbell in Kentucky, the same hangar we'd departed from. There was a band and we marched in. My mom, dad, and younger brother Dylan were there, and so was my girlfriend, Kristine. They gave us about two minutes to see our families before loading us up on buses to take us back to the battalion company area. We secured our weapons and were released about four hours later to spend time with family. We were allowed to come in late the next day and then went home on leave for two weeks.

It was hard. You go from working a twenty-hour day in the most rigorous conditions to having family ask, "Hey, can we have lunch tomorrow?" You get to sleep in a building that doesn't have a leaky roof, and you're showered and wearing clean clothes, not camouflage. It's kind of overwhelming. I remember thinking I wanted to just go to a place with a lot of people and sit and watch, to slowly assimilate back into the world. I didn't want to talk and answer questions. But I did anyway, for everyone else.

When I look back at photos from the day I returned, I see a different person in the picture. He was a sober kid, hollow eyed. Even though I am smiling, I was numb inside, a small piece of me had died. I received a lot of slaps on the back for some of the things I did in that 2003 invasion, but I was just doing my job. It left me with some emotional baggage I'll have to carry the rest of my life. The tour's over, but it's never really over.

CHAPTER 14

Stop-Loss

After returning from our first tour in 2004, we all went in different directions. Some got out of the Army—they'd had enough, others transferred to different units. Some took other assignments, such as drill sergeants or recruiters. A few of us stayed in the Rakkasans, and I started working my way through the ranks. When we heard everyone talking about a second deployment in 2005, I didn't think I'd be returning. I had five years and 337 days in, and since I'd signed on for six years, my time was up. Then they hit me with the bad news: "Murph, you're not getting out. You're going back."

I didn't think it was possible. "I signed for six years, and I'm going to go ahead and go home. I have a great girlfriend and a wonderful family and a lot of opportunity."

They explained, "You don't understand, you're not going home." There was a shortage of troops, and the Army had instituted their stop-loss policy, which meant they could force me to stay.

I called my dad and told him the problem. He was insistent. "Son, come home." I reminded him that if I came home, I would get a dishonorable discharge. I couldn't believe his response. Mr. Pro-American Marine told me, "A man's got to stand for something, and you stood for this country when it asked you to. They're not living up to their side of the deal."

At this point, I had been promoted to a sergeant E5 acting as a staff sergeant and was in charge of eleven guys on an infantry reconnaissance squad. After I hung up the phone, I started thinking about

those men. Half of them had never been to war. I thought about everything I had seen, and I felt this sense of duty and service. I called my
dad back and said, "Dad, I'm not going to leave these guys. I'm going."
I didn't want to go, of course, but I wasn't going to abandon them.

* * *

The previous year, the Army had decided to make a few changes in
our structure. In order to make infantry brigades more lethal, they
wanted cavalry elements placed in them—what came to be known
RSTAs: reconnaissance, surveillance, target acquisition teams. Basically, they would be giving the infantry heavier mechanized equipment, like Bradleys with better night vision, because we couldn't carry
these massive FLIRs (forward-looking infrared cameras). The cavalry
scouts already had this technology using Bradleys, so they thought it
would be great to bring them over to our unit, too.

In the infantry world, you have a division, brigade, battalion,
company, platoon, squad, and then team. To accomplish this goal, the
new plan proposed we do away with our Third Battalion. Well, the
Rakkasans went crazy, because the Third Battalion is the most decorated battalion. They eventually worked out a compromise. The Third
Battalion picked up their gear and moved in with the Second Battalion, and a cavalry regiment called 1-33rd CAV started forming in the
former Third Battalion area. The Second Battalion (in name) went
away, and now there was just the First, 3rd, and 1-33rd CAV—all Rakkasans. This new unit had an Alpha Troop (not a company), a Bravo
Troop, and a Charlie Company, with Charlie run by an infantry commander and emphasizing reconnaissance.

While merging infantry with cavalry may have looked good from
the twenty-thousand-foot level, something that was not taken into

account was the culture of infantry. We do not mesh well with others, except maybe the medics. They were our brothers; they're not any different. Marines are the same way—they love their Navy corpsmen. They're equal, not below. But in the infantry, you have to believe you're the best because you have the hardest mission, and you have to believe that everybody else is your support, because they are. It takes a lot to get an infantryman on the ground.

Cavalry scouts didn't understand that; they tended to think that they were equal to us, and we just didn't agree. In this new mix, it was very apparent that we didn't want to work with them and they didn't want to work with us. We had never trained with them, we had never cross-trained with them—we didn't even know *how* to cross-train with them.

I could kind of see how the leadership thought it was a good idea, but they didn't give us enough time to learn how to deal with each other, and they never gave us a mission where we trained together. Sure, I might have been on a hundred missions with cavalry scouts previously and didn't know it, because I was so wrapped up in my infantry mission, but it was part of a bigger mission that the colonels and battalion commanders were operating, and I just didn't see it. But to my knowledge, I never cross-trained with any of those guys.

But the change did bring some opportunity. They were recruiting for the reconnaissance element, and I started thinking about it. A lot of my buddies were going over to the new Third Battalion, and I could have stayed with them and continued doing the same work, but I had always romanticized being on my own, being in a scout-style environment. It wasn't infantry, it wasn't what I had been trained to do, but it more closely resembled my fighting style—guerrilla warfare. I always loved deer hunting, being still in a tree all day waiting for a buck to come by. That fit me better than the "Rah-rah-rah. Left, left,

left. Machine guns! Charge!" which I had been doing for years. I was tired of it. I knew that reconnaissance would be a lot harder and more physically demanding, but I could do it. I wasn't like the extreme studs who were going to get picked, but I thought I was good enough and it wouldn't be too torturous for me.

First Sergeant James Coroy was given the 1-33rd CAV Charlie Company, and you had to audition for a spot. Coroy had served in four combat deployments, including Desert Storm and Afghanistan. He'd received all kinds of awards and medals and would be a tough one to please. He shared the company with a really impressive commander, Captain Sean McGee. McGee was very knowledgeable, very confident, very calculating. He knew his job, and he was always in character. There was never any joking around with McGee, not for guys like me or lower. During the combatives part of the Week of the Eagle competition—the Ultimate Fighting Championship portion of the event—he took second out of the whole division, roughly thirty-five thousand men. Every company sends their best, and he had to compete on the brigade and battalion levels before the division level. I remember cheering him on at the fight, which was a cross between wrestling and judo, almost like jujitsu. I had a lot of respect for him. If you can be the strongest of the strong, be humble, and also back it up, that's impressive to me.

I told Coroy I was interested in recon, and he said, "Yeah, right, Murph. You can forget it. You're going over to Second Battalion." That's just how he is. I knew he wanted me to back down and say I was joking, that I didn't really mean it. He wanted to see how bad I wanted it. So I said, "All right. I just wanted you to know. I'm going for it." Right there, he knew I was serious. So I got called into his office for an interview.

Coroy was looking at three things: One was physical training (PT). Were you good enough, strong enough, fast enough? Two, had you ever been in any trouble? Three, could you shoot well? Fortunately, my PT stayed above average. It wasn't the highest, but it was near perfect on the Army's scale. In order to be excellent, you had to have to have a 270 out of 300. I was always around a 290, and I made 300 a few times. My reputation was stellar, too, and I could always shoot.

When I arrived at Coroy's office, his attitude had changed. He knew little things about me, but he had never worked with me directly, because he was on a much higher level. He knew I'd been in the Rak-kasans. Coroy knew I was a smartass and that I drove a big, black F-250 diesel, and he knew that after the company party the previous year there were nine knuckleheads who wouldn't leave, and I scooped them up, put them in my truck, and got some beautiful girl to drive us all home. I'm sure he thought I was a little odd, unconventional compared to the other guys.

He might have mistakenly thought I was a rich kid. A lot of my buddies in the Army thought that because I had a nice truck and my play vehicle was a tricked-out '78 Jeep CJ-7 with a V8 engine. I bought it in Nashville for thirty-five hundred dollars cash. But I saved for it. I was smart with my money; I invested it. I did things that made sense. I didn't get tattoos, I didn't eat out every night—I cooked instead. The truth is that I did not come from a wealthy family. The most valuable thing my dad gave me was an education on how to save money.

Now First Sergeant Coroy had my PT score and my last Non-commissioned Officer Evaluation Report, so at least that put me in the running. I'm sure he had plenty of other guys on his A-list. In his mind, I was not one of them. He suspected I would not stay in the Army, and therefore I was not one of the guys worth focusing a lot of time and energy on. The guys who stayed in the Army and made that clear to the leadership were constantly being groomed and sent to great schools. Leaders don't want to waste a lot of effort on guys like me.

The original list for this company was probably 150, and they could take 100. I had given it a lot of thought. If I made it, it would be a big deal because I had already been with the original Third Battalion, 187th Infantry Regiment, which was now disbanded. I was looking for a new challenge. The recon would be experimental for me, a chance to be part of something special. Maybe my last hurrah.

I made the cut. Even better, I earned one of the six squad leader positions. By that time, I had done all the jobs. I'd worked as a SAW gunner, bravo team leader, and alpha team leader. I was a squad leader for a year and a half, even though I didn't have the rank to go with it. I was an E5 acting as an E6. Because I was a squad leader, if another E5 said something smart to me, I could technically make him do push-ups. Of course, I would. If you said something that I didn't like, I could either challenge you to a fight or just make you do something, and you've got to do it. You can't have guys push you around and have someone else see it. If they see that you can be owned, it could be bad.

So I made it into the recon company and was proud. I knew the other guys Coroy and McGee had picked, and they were all studs. In the infantry, you have guys who signed up and wanted to be there, and they were like your Marines. Then you had guys who signed up just to get the hell out of wherever they were from, and they were good soldiers. And then you had guys who played video games and romanticized about being infantrymen but really didn't have what it took. Those were our problem guys. We had to spend a lot more time with our problem children. They got injured, they got in trouble. Sometimes they just weren't physically gifted so they couldn't keep up the pace. They were the ones you had to constantly ride.

But this new group was handpicked. There weren't going to be any guys who couldn't run extremely fast or do all the physical requirements. And more than likely, these guys weren't going to be caught doing drugs or getting into trouble. They were there because they wanted to be there, and they were the cream of the crop. And I was going to be lucky enough to lead eleven of them.

We had three platoons with only two squads in each. Our whole mission was to never be seen. And if we did get into a scrap, our mission was to live to fight another day. We would try to kill the enemy quickly and then get out of there. We would be doing a lot without really doing a lot: we would be providing key information and already be in place when the infantry came. We might be sniping the enemy's officers or those jackasses who were putting IEDs in the ground.

I had nine guys assigned to me initially, and right before we deployed they fleshed us out with some 19 Deltas (cavalry scouts). Adam Jefferson was one of them. After basic training, he received orders to the 101st Airborne Division and was confused. He was a 19 Delta, not infantry, and he had not yet heard about the Army's new RSTAs. We couldn't understand why we were getting 19 Deltas, either; it just seemed ridiculous. They don't even go to our basic training. They don't get any infantry training, and now here they're going to be infantry scouts. It was just unfathomable.

Jefferson was one of nine privates who were waiting upstairs, and I was supposed to get two from the group. The word was circling around downstairs among the infantry scouts that our new guys had arrived. Like a band of fraternity brothers waiting to haze, some of our guys were slamming metal lockers, making barking noises and yelling, "Cherries!" They couldn't wait to initiate them, a process that could go on for more than a year.

I went upstairs to meet them. A lot of the squad leaders were older than me. I was one of the youngest, so I slid into the company area and was able to observe them before they knew it. They were standing in parade rest, arms behind their backs, feet shoulder-width apart. I studied them and tried to detect their flaws. I was looking for somebody who was physically fit for an eighteen-year-old coming from basic training. I realized they were going to be a little on the light side but knew we could beef them up. I was looking for somebody who didn't appear nervous. They were scared to death, of course, so I checked to see whose head was straight and whose eyes were dancing around the room. Were they trying to look pitiful so someone wouldn't mess with them? Or were they too cocky, a little too comfortable in this situation? I was looking for the right mixture. I studied their uniforms to see whose was squared away. They had anticipated coming that day, so I knew their hearts were beating out of their chests. They didn't really belong there—they weren't infantry—so that had to add to the fear.

There was a really big guy named Flowers. He looked strong, and I was hoping he wasn't too cocky. Then there was Jefferson, who was relatively short—about five eight—but I could tell he was strong. He was square jawed, broad at the shoulders, and looked like a little machine.

Someone finally pointed me out to the group—"This guy right here is one of your potential squad leaders"—probably trying to scare them. They all looked at me, and I gave them a smirk, like, *You guys are going to be eaten alive, but it ain't going to be me who does it.* Someone yelled an order, and they all hit the floor doing push-ups. I saw a few knock out fifty, sixty, seventy. Some had gone too fast and didn't realize how long they'd be down there. They gave it everything they had and then stopped. Jefferson was still pushing. I told him, "You! Get up. Go stand over there." I asked the rest of them where they were from. One said, "Indiana." Another said, "Ohio." The big one said, "Georgia." I told him, "You, go stand over there with him." I turned to the guy with the clipboard and said, "I'll take these two." About that time, the other squad leader came in, and I could tell he was mad because I had first choice. He was much older than me and had been a staff sergeant a long time, but he had to take the ones I left.

I pulled Jefferson and Flowers into the hallway and told them quietly, "I'll be cooler to you guys than any other squad leader in this company, but the first time you mess up, I'm going to come down on you like a hammer." Jefferson took those words to heart. He never wanted to make a mistake for that reason. That's all I wanted them to do. I wanted them to believe that I would kill them, but that I'd give them as much rope as they needed. A lot of guys hung themselves from that rope, but not Jefferson. Every time he did something right, I praised him in front of everybody. He seemed to appreciate that I gave him a fair shot.

Both these men would end up being in the convoy with me the night of the blast.

CHAPTER 15

Differences

Despite my reluctance to do a second tour, since I'd expected to get out, at least this time around I had rank. Most of the guys who had my rank were in their late twenties and early thirties, while I was still in my early twenties. There was a reason I valued rank. I didn't like people being in charge of me. I tried really hard to have as few people over me as possible, and of course the way you did that was through making rank. Because I was in charge of a squad, I was able to dictate a little bit what I did and what they did. It made it more interesting and less stressful. Maybe it was because I was given more knowledge. To me, not knowing is the worst.

In the Army, there are different leadership styles. For example, in the Special Forces selection process, they don't yell at you and scream at you. It's all professional, no screaming. I've never experienced it personally, but I've talked to a lot of guys who have. As a squad leader, I tried to treat my recon guys more like that, straight professionals, more like a civilian workforce than regular infantry. My leadership hated it; they wanted me to be like the old me, which was rah-rah infantry. I just felt like I could get the same results without it. Any time my leadership wasn't watching or evaluating me, I was an entirely different squad leader. I didn't let my team leaders run things the old way, either. I told them how I wanted things done. I mean, if they messed up the slightest bit, I hammered them, absolutely. But I wasn't their drill sergeant. I gave them plenty of slack and tried to understand who they were and what they were capable of. We needed them, especially considering what was waiting for us in Iraq.

There's an advantage to knowing as much as you can about your guys, down to knowing what they look like when they move at night. I could tell every one of my men by the way they walked, their unique profile. I knew their breaking points, their weaknesses. It wasn't something that every leader did, but it was important to me to get to know as much as I could about their world, their motivations. You've got to know every single thing about a person when you're building a team. Especially when people's lives depend on your leadership.

That first tour, I had no idea what to expect, and my leadership was in chaos because they didn't know what to expect, either. Everyone was always screaming, and information was never passed down.

On my second tour, I wanted my guys to know as much as possible, and I wanted them to *want* to know. Of course, they would sometimes take advantage of this approach and use it to complain about some of my training. I'd say to them, "Guys, on my last tour…" and they would mock me. "Oh, great, here we go again." But I wanted them to know how terrible it was when things were just forced on us.

Probably the biggest lesson for me on my first tour was learning how *not* to do things. That helped shape my leadership style. I told them, "I'll be a democratic leader. I want to know your opinions, but at the end, I am going to be the one to make the decision." In war, you have to be an authoritative leader. It's "Do what I say *now*; don't ask why." But I could be both authoritative and democratic.

I told them I wanted to know what they thought. "In combat, I want to know what you're seeing. If you see a guy with an RPG, don't assume that I saw him because I'm the boss and I'm this awesome guy. No, you tell me what you're seeing—every little thing. Don't be afraid." Some guys in the regular infantry are afraid to speak up, so I was trying to do things a little different.

I felt a lot of appreciation from the guys for my approach. I think they even hoped nothing would happen to me, because if they got another squad leader, he might not take care of them the way I did. I got a reputation in the company of being more approachable because I didn't yell a lot and I respected them; I wanted to know where they were from, what they did in high school. I let them know what to expect when told to be in formation at five thirty—I explained that the other squad leaders were going to have their men lined up at four thirty or five, so they'd better be early. Everything I did was on their behalf, which earned their loyalty. And the rest of the company noticed.

A lot of guys knew if they saw me walking, they could say hello, unlike with some others—you didn't dare to even look their way. I was more approachable. That's one of the reasons it was so hard on some of the company when I got wounded. Several of the guys who were on my squad in infantry went full sprint running up to see who was wounded. They said, "It's not Murphy. Tell me it's not Murph." And they were told, "It's Murph."

Some of the toughest guys in the company and other platoons cried because we'd had a relationship in the past. I was their squad leader or their team leader or they just respected me. They took it hard.

* * *

We did a lot of pretty sweet training before the second deployment. We went down to Louisiana, and the Army brought in Iraqis to make the setting more realistic. They had mock villages set up, and the people would yell at us. In my mind, it was like a terrible B movie, but I guess for the guys who had never been there before it was the most real thing they'd ever seen.

We were more specific in our training, too. We weren't all over the board training for everything and for the unknowns, which we'd faced in 2003. We had no idea what to expect back then. Now, we had the advantage of past experience, information being passed on from the battlefield. We knew the situation on the ground. We knew to train for patrolling in Humvees, patrolling on foot, patrolling in an urban theater. On top of that was our reconnaissance training, learning methods of sneaking in and out of places and not being seen. And how to collect information and pass it to higher-ups, who would in turn pass it to regular infantry guys who would go in and crush the enemy.

Training helped everyone get in sync, but especially the new guys like Jefferson. I was in a similar situation on my first tour—unprepared. But he had an advantage over me through the countless training missions. There wasn't a lot of time for that back in '03. It was less chaotic for Jefferson, too, compared to those who served earlier in Iraq. At the time of my first tour, there was a lot of pressure on the higher-ups because of all the unknowns. There was a lot of uncertainty about whether Saddam Hussein would use chemical weapons. We had no reason to think he wouldn't, since we were invading his country. And he had used nerve gas previously on the Kurds and on his own people, so that was at the forefront of our minds. We were all over-stressed because leadership had no idea what they were sending their men into.

There was none of that in 2005. Most of us had already been to Iraq, some of us had been in Afghanistan, and we learned from those experiences. Our unit was also getting guys from other units of the Army who had served in the Middle East, and they brought a different perspective. There was a lot of knowledge coming from the battleground, too, so we'd have an idea where we might be working and what we might be doing. We had more insight on how to prepare. It was much more professional in my opinion.

Before my second tour, we were sent home for our final leave to wind up our personal business prior to departure. This was late August, and Florida had been getting hammered with hurricanes. On August 25, Hurricane Katrina made landfall as a Category 1 hurricane in southeast Florida, but my hometown was spared. It was downgraded to a tropical storm, then slammed into the Louisiana-Mississippi coast as a Category 3 hurricane four days later. After the levees were breached and eighty-five percent of New Orleans flooded, there was mass chaos at the Superdome, and a number of our guys were affected. They had families in the area, some of whom had lost homes or had to evacuate and feared their homes were underwater. But the war wouldn't wait, so they returned to Fort Campbell to prepare for deployment to Iraq.

The day before we deployed, First Sergeant Coroy grabbed me and asked, "Where's your new ID card, Murphy?" I had been told I needed a new one because my current ID card said my time was up in a few weeks.

I responded, "I don't have one yet, First Sergeant. I've been a little busy getting ready for deployment," which was kind of a cocky answer.

He said, "You will get a goddamn ID card and show it to me by the end of the day."

I replied, "Yes, First Sergeant." Coroy was right, I needed the ID, but it pissed me off. Getting a new ID card with the word "indefinite" was going to be a total morale killer. My whole career, I had been looking at my ID card with the date I was getting out: October 1, 2005. Now, all of a sudden, that date was null and void.

As much as I didn't like it, I told my platoon sergeant about the order and headed to the division-level ID card office. It was kind of like the DMV, only one hundred times worse. I sat in lines all day. I kept thinking, *I can't believe I'm deploying to Iraq tomorrow.* I was growing angrier by the minute because this was not a good use of my time, and the people behind the counter—POAGs—had attitudes. *They* weren't about to go to Iraq tomorrow; they didn't even know what stop-loss was. After nearly nine hours, I finally got the new card and headed back to work. It was the end of the day, so everybody was gone. I didn't have family in Fort Campbell, so I just made phone calls and finished putting things in storage.

The flight to Iraq was smoother this time—and it was free of creepy flight attendants. I kept my team leaders at a close distance and made sure they knew exactly what to do. I also checked behind them when they weren't looking. In the military, the only way to know something is actually done is to go look yourself. If possible, I would always do that. You have to. It's not a micromanaging thing, it's just I can't risk giving a false order. If I tell somebody something got done based on someone telling me it got done and it wasn't done, I'm the one who's going to get fired. Even though it's not technically my fault, I should have gone and checked.

Passing information down the line went like this: The leadership would pull all the platoon sergeants and lieutenants aside and brief them, and then they'd call for their squad leaders and brief us, and then we would brief the team leaders, who would brief the men. I operated a little differently. I just told all the men everything directly. That way I knew they got the information. I wouldn't have to wonder if some team leader cherry-picked information, which mine had done to me when I was a Joe. If something was really important, I wanted to say it to everybody. If it was something small, like, "Don't forget to bring an extra pair of socks," then the team leaders could do it. But if it was really important, I'd make sure everybody had their pen and paper, and I'd put the information out. It turned out that I didn't need to worry about it. Erik Roberts and Brian Black were excellent team leaders.

This time we flew into Baghdad International Airport (BIAP). Everybody had been calling it "By-op," and I finally figured it out and said, "Oh, when I was here in OIF1 (Operation Iraqi Freedom), it was called Saddam International Airport." Some of the guys rolled their eyes, like, *Oh, god, here we go again. He's going to tell another OIF1 story.* The new guys get so tired of hearing about previous combat experiences. It felt like when a kid says, "Shut up, Dad," as he starts to hear his father tell a story for the fiftieth time.

But the last time I was there it was called Saddam International, and our first mission had been to clear it. It had had a big picture of Hussein's ugly face, but that was gone now. This BIAP place now had a Taco Bell and a Burger King and barricades around the campus to stop suicide bombers. It was a major post, the American military hub in Iraq. Marines went there, SEALs went there, and it was where all the big equipment was flown in then reappropriated. There were maybe twenty thousand to thirty thousand servicemen and women working out of forty buildings. It had a PX, a military exchange store where you could get gear and groceries, even a TV. But it was POAG central, so our leaders wanted us out of that place and into combat as soon as possible. We didn't need to be around all those softies who were walking around with Snickers bars and calling home four times a day and who would eventually return to the States and brag that they'd been to Iraq even though they'd never left the BIAP.

* * *

When we arrived in theater, they decided to send some of the leaders into the city first to learn the area, learn the roads, and communicate everything to their men. So the platoon sergeants and lieutenants stayed back with our Joes at BIAP while the other squad leaders and I were flown by helicopter to a National Guard operating base in Samarra.

When you go into a city, you're expected to know it inside and out the first day. Sometimes it's a city the size of Boston, and you've got to know it from day one. It's not possible, of course, but we were there doing the "right-seat rides" in an armored Humvee anyway. On my second day in-country, I was scanning the streets, studying the people, smelling the trash that was burning on the side of the road, listening to the Muslim call to prayer, feeling the dry desert heat, and thinking, *It's just like last time. Nothing's changed.* I was in the back left seat, and after we made a few turns, I looked to my left and saw a vehicle. I noticed the driver was really clean-shaven, just a bit *too* clean-shaven, I thought. Then about two or three seconds later, I heard *kaboom*, a big friggin' explosion. I remember thinking, *Now that's different from last time.*

I saw a torso fly above our vehicle and skid across the road—there were no legs. I thought it must be the gunner of the truck behind us. I didn't know him because I was with a different unit; I was just here to learn the roads. It turned out that the torso belonged to a suicide bomber, and it had flown from a truck that was loaded down with artillery rounds the size of traffic cones. Each one is about a hundred pounds, and just one of them will kill everything within fifty yards. He was loaded down with six. During my previous tour, we did not have to face IEDs—improvised explosive devices. This was a vehicle-borne IED. A suicide bomber will get clean-shaven, put on his best clothes, and then go see his seventy-two virgins after the explosion—that's what these people believe. So it registered with me when I saw that the guy looked a little too cleaned up.

I heard voices screaming over the radios, the National Guards, and looked out my window to try to figure out what had happened. We kept rolling down the road, and I thought, *My company is not even here yet, they're all back at the BIAP eating Taco Bell, and they almost lost two of their squad leaders.* Our driver floored it and went about a half a mile and then parked. We got out of the trucks and looked around for IEDs but didn't find any. The Humvee that had been hit was coming toward us. Two of our guys were in it, two of our squad leaders, Staff Sergeant Steve Denzer and Staff Sergeant Patrick Cook. The truck was slowly limping our way, like in one of those eerie movies.

After a blast, civilians panic. They run and hide. They think we're going to come kill everybody in retaliation. Then things get really quiet. Because it's the desert, dust hangs in the air for a while, then slowly settles. The wind seems to stop or at least slow down.

That Humvee was doing all it could to keep going, but the engine sounded horrible and there was liquid blowing out the bottom of it. The windows were all white from the effects of the blast—it looked like it had been shot at a thousand times with a shotgun. The blast didn't break the windows, but it spidered them to the point that you couldn't see out. The vehicle was smoky looking and black. All the tires were shredded, and I noticed that the gunner was not up in the turret. Fifty miles an hour is pretty fast for a Humvee with all the armor on it, but this thing was creeping up at maybe ten miles an hour. It was revved as high as it could go. Our Humvees usually have three or four ten-foot whip antennas for the radios. You need to stay connected to the battalion, the brigade, and your company. There's a different antenna for each one. It's pretty easy for the bad guys to figure out which vehicle holds officers because officers ride around in trucks with ten friggin' antennas. I'm not sure how many this truck had at the time of the blast, but all of them were blown off.

When the doors opened on the vehicle, smoke came billowing out. Everyone was covered in soot from the blast. The gunner, a National Guardsman, was lying on the seat. He had been injured. Denzer looked like he was okay, just pissed off and covered in soot, so I went up to Cook. He seemed out of it.

Cook is a little taller than me and wider in the shoulders. I looked him in the face and said, "Are you all right, Cook?" He said, "Yeah, yeah, I'm fine." I thought he might have a concussion. I took his weapon from him. I pulled it out of his hand and dropped the magazine and pulled the charger back and ejected the shell and caught it. I loaded his clip, put it in his vest, buttoned it down—velcroed it down, really—then gave him his weapon back. "Just hang out, buddy." Then I said, "Let me clean your glasses." I grabbed his yellow shooting glasses and started cleaning the black soot off of them, just trying to comfort him with simple things.

All of a sudden, he snapped out of it and looked at me, then pulled his magazine out and slammed it in his weapon; he loaded it. I explained, "I was just clearing your weapon. I don't know where your head is at." But his reaction told me that at least he could pull security if there was about to be a fight. I could count on him; he was ready to roll.

Before that moment, Cook and I had been rivals, since we were both squad leaders. There wasn't any animosity, just friendly competition. But months later, he came up to me at our operating base and said, "Remember that second day when we got blown up and you came up and cleared my weapon?" I'd felt kind of awkward about it, especially after he reloaded it. He said, "You know, that was the right thing to do. I just want you to know that it was smart that you did that. Good thinking." *Oh, all right.* That's all we said, and he walked away. It had been weighing on him, I guess. It had not been a big deal to me; I just didn't want him to have an accident.

We finally got the full story. The gunner had seen the suicide bomber heading toward our convoy and fired a warning shot with a 9mm pistol, but the bomber kept coming. The gunner didn't have time to switch to the machine gun, so he kept firing into the driver's windshield. It was clear the Iraqi was trying to T-bone their Humvee and blow it, which would have shot the vehicle into the air and killed all five men inside. I don't know if the gunner's bullets actually hit the driver, causing the bombs to blow too soon, or what, but they detonated fifteen feet early, which was enough distance to save everyone, but the shrapnel went everywhere, and the gunner was injured because he was in the turret still shooting. He was one of their best, he had done a really good job, and he received a Purple Heart for it. So did Cook.

A little girl had been standing on the side of the road in front of her house when the guy detonated his vehicle, so they evacuated her with the gunner and Cook, who had a burn on his chest, to the aid station just a few miles down the road. While Cook was waiting in the stretcher, he watched the medics giving the little girl CPR, trying to save her life. He watched her die. I could tell it bothered him. Some of the leaders went to the girl's funeral and tried to speak to the family and offer condolences, to ask if there was anything we could do, but the family blamed us for her death. Even though we got blown up, too! They just didn't get it.

My men eventually showed up; they had heard what happened. They were glad that I was okay. This was the second day; I realized it was going to be a long damn tour. It was going to be a tough go. I just didn't know how tough.

CHAPTER 16

Blue Door Alley

We started doing a lot of offensive maneuvers, a lot of raids. The days went by, the weeks went by, there were minor skirmishes here and there. Someone told me they were holding a Staff Sergeant Board, so I went to it and was finally promoted to staff sergeant.

We operated out of a three-story building that had been a casino. It was about five acres, and the National Guards named it Patrol Base Olson, in honor of Army Staff Sergeant Todd Olson from Wisconsin, who was killed in 2004 when his vehicle was hit by a roadside bomb in Samarra. Our guys were given a sandbagged position at the top, where we could see down into the city. There was no elevator, of course, so we were constantly hauling our weapons and equipment up and down three flights of stairs.

Three of our platoons operated out of the base, and we were in charge of security for the building. We rotated guys through observation posts. One of them, observation post number four, looked down into one of the main avenues of the city. At the very center, where the road stopped, was the Golden Dome Mosque of Samarra, about four football field lengths away. About midway down the road, there was an alley to the left where people walked to get to the main intersection, and in the alley was a huge blue door, so we called it Blue Door Alley. The National Guards told us they were constantly taking fire from it but had no way to fight back. They said bad guys knew they could shoot from that position without being seen, then run. They were gone before we could get to them.

We later learned that the mafia types who ran the casino we were now using as our operating base were paying people to shoot at us. They said it had nothing to do with jihad or their beliefs. It was business to them; it was about money. The Americans screwed up their whole trade. We were living in their casino, we had roadblocks all over the place, and they couldn't do their mafia-style business because of US forces. So they kept trying to blow us up and kill us because they hated our guts; we'd affected their livelihood.

One day while patrolling near the mosque, which was right across from Blue Door Alley, I saw an empty room on the second story of a building. It was an abandoned, junked-out adobe-style loft above a shop. There were holes in the roof, and it obviously hadn't been used in a while. It probably wasn't even livable. I pointed it out to Erik Roberts and said, "Take a look at that," because it looked right down Blue Door Alley. Basically, to your left would be OP4. To your right would be the mosque. You could see right down the alley. I was thinking if we could put a sniper in there, when that little knucklehead came in the middle of the night trying to get ten bucks from the mafia for shooting at us, we could put him to sleep forever.

I mentioned it to my lieutenant, and he wrote it up as a mission and submitted it to the commander for consideration. They called me in and thought it was a good idea. It was the first offensive sniper mission of our tour. It would be my mission, and I was going to bring a sniper, a sniper spotter, and two of my guys—five of us total. That's a little heavy for a hide, but it was about the only way I was going to convince the leadership to let us go. Two guys is kind of scary. You can get overrun. That's the traditional sniper way, but it's just hard to sell to your commander if he's not really on board. So I knew I could get away with three to five guys for that type of mission.

The plan was for us to go on the same type of patrol we had gone on the day I discovered the loft, go into a shop, maybe bring thirty guys in and thirty guys out. Then skip two shops and go to another one, same thing. The patrol would be cover for our real objective; the whole time the real mission was to get to Blue Door Alley and have thirty guys go in and twenty-five come out, and hope that the Iraqis didn't notice.

So we finally went into the building. It was totally abandoned, like I suspected. It was right at dusk. We lay on our bellies until it got dark. We knew the Iraqis below us pulled down the gates and locked up their shops around five p.m. The whole time we were up there above them, we weren't allowed to move. We only had five guys, so we could easily be outnumbered or overpowered if someone was able to get a shot at us with a rocket-propelled grenade (RPG).

Once they all left, the street slowed down and we were able to start moving around a little bit. We used a hole in the roof for the radio antenna and established communications back to OP4. Those guys would communicate back to the company level, where the officers would be standing by. It was kind of cool knowing that the whole company was paying attention to our mission. More than anything, I wanted to wax these idiots who had been tormenting the National Guard and make sure they weren't going to shoot at my men, either.

We set up a perfect spot right on a window, looking down over the alley. We ran mosquito netting straight down from the ceiling, over the window, and then we put a second sheet up at the top of the ceiling and ran it back toward the shooter, who would be five or six feet behind the window, at an angle. With this effect, you could basically see out perfectly but nobody could see in. We were in total noise and light discipline mode at this point. Every movement we made had to be like a ninja. Everything we did had to be slow, methodical, and thought-out. Every bit of trash that we accumulated from food would have to be taken out with us. Therefore, everything they brought in, I knew about. Everything they were going to take out, I would know about. I would be the last one out of the hide in a few days to make sure we didn't leave any trash, or else that position would be totally compromised, and if we decided to do another mission, it could be rigged to blow.

We had comms, we had the camouflage netting on the window, and it was getting dark. I found a spot at the corner of the room and was using a tool to hollow out an opening, creating another shooting lane toward the mosque. We could see right down Blue Door Alley on the first shooting lane, but if anybody went to the right, we wouldn't be able to get a shot on them. I was opening up this crack so I could see the mosque.

Finally, it was dark, and we couldn't have any lights on, so we used our night vision and whatever natural light was in the room. We were filthy from being on the floor and sliding around like snakes. We knew at first light the shop owners would all come back, and we wouldn't be able to make any movement for another full day. We were moving around stealth-like because everything you do in the city travels. If a guy lights a cigarette, you could hear the match strike for hundreds of meters. So everything—everything—was very calculated.

My shooter was set up with an M24 sniper rifle, which is basically a model 700 Remington 308 with a heavy barrel. It's free-floating and a little bit tricked out for the snipers in the military and snipers in law enforcement. The butt stock is self-adjustable to the shooter. It comes with a bullet-drop compensated Leupold scope for daytime. The settings on the scope were really intense. If the target was at a thousand meters, you would just put it on ten and pull the trigger and that sucker was dead. It did all the math for you. The weapon was obviously all camoed out and looked really good. The sniper carrying it had been to sniper school at Fort Benning, Georgia. He was one of the studs in our company.

Once it got dark, I told everybody to go ahead and get some sleep. They looked at me like, "No, dude, we're not tired." But they did it anyway; they knew they'd have to pull shifts later. Probably the main reason I wanted them to go to sleep was that I wanted to be the guy at the trigger when that idiot came out. I kept a guy awake to monitor the radio, shifting hourly. I watched a few hours, then woke another guy up, and he watched, but I stayed up and kept watch, too. Then he went to sleep, and I woke another guy up. I stayed up and watched. At some point, everybody had been up, but I put everybody down again except for the radio guy.

On this watch, I saw a guy walk into the street, way up by the Golden Dome Mosque. I saw him through the crack I had made with my little metal tool. There was a curfew in effect and there was no walking in the city after nine p.m. This guy was out past curfew, carrying an AK-47, and staying just outside of OP4's view.

I kicked the foot of the guy next to me and saw his eyes open. He didn't move. He didn't make a noise, just turned toward me and I gave him a look. He kicked the guy next to him and he woke up. Then he kicked the guy next to him, and finally everybody was awake. Roberts came to me, and I told him, "I've got one guy out in the road looking around. I don't know what he's doing, but just get everybody up and spread the word. Get the radio guy and make sure he's on whisper mode on the microphone. Have him do a comm check with OP4 and ask if they see this guy standing down here in the road." So they did all that. I kept my eye on him, and I lined the scope right on this dude. At this point, it would be a sixty-yard shot with a rifle that shoots over a thousand meters. It's a chip shot.

My radio guy was having trouble communicating because they wanted him to speak up, but they didn't understand that we were in a hide. In whisper mode, your voice comes across muffled, but loud, so they can hear you even if you're speaking low.

I heard a helicopter coming, which made sense because we were in a war zone where our choppers were flying all the time. I saw the guy on the ground looking for the chopper, too. I was looking at him through the M24's night vision scope. It was green, but I could see every move he was making. I saw him looking up for the chopper, then run across the street. I thought, *That dude is hiding, he's acting nervous.* The next thing you know, he was back in the middle of the street. He signaled to the other side, and two guys ran across the road. I thought, *Yes! All right, now we're in business.* I looked a little farther and saw another guy with an AK-47. All the while that chopper was still doing something in the distance.

I heard the chopper coming closer, and I was zeroing in on the guy by the mosque. Suddenly, he dove under a big dumpster. These were not very common in Iraq; you hardly ever saw them. It looked like it might be for construction trash. They were always doing construction on the mosque. When he got under the dumpster, I knew— that's enough. But I had to get permission to shoot, since this wasn't our primary mission. If a guy had been sitting in front of me smoking the OP4 tower, then I could shoot him, but this was different.

So I put another guy on the weapon and slid over to the radio. I called back and said, "Shadow CP, this is Shadow 3-2. Over." They came back, "Shadow 3-2, this is Shadow CP." This is the command center where they've got big maps and all these dots and pins. They've got all the frequencies. They radioed messages for the commander. I knew there'd be an officer awake on duty, probably a lieutenant, because it was late at night and the commander would be sleeping. I asked to speak to whoever was in charge. That person got on the mic, and I said, "This is Shadow 3-2." I heard, "What's up, Murph?"

I said, "I've got three individuals with weapons down near the mosque. I think they're bad guys."

He came back, "Why do you think they're bad guys?"

I told them my reasoning. He asked me to repeat, which I had to do several times. Finally, OP4 was trying to cut in, because they knew what I was saying, and they were trying to tell the person in charge. I wanted the command post to wake up the commander because they wouldn't give me permission to shoot.

I completely understood their thinking. There were cops that patrolled around the mosque, and they didn't want me shooting any friendlies. But I knew this was different; these jokers were up to no good. One of the guys carrying a weapon had a bag. I had never seen an Iraqi carrying anything shaped like this—it looked almost like the kind you use to haul bats to a baseball game, about half the size of a golf bag. It was long and skinny and had a handle at the center.

They didn't give me permission to shoot, and I didn't shoot them. The next day, they were thinking of pulling us out. I told them I wanted to stay another day and night. I asked the guys if they were all right staying, and even though we'd barely stood up, they said they were willing. I told them we'd been close the previous night, so let's give it another try.

I wanted to get these guys, and I wanted to get them bad. They shot at us all the time, and we never got to kill them because they wouldn't stick around. They would pop around corners when we were on patrol and spray us. Maybe if you could see them, you could get a couple of shots, but they usually just sprayed quickly and ran.

We ended up staying three days and three nights, which was longer than we were supposed to, and they had to drag me out of there.

They kept saying, "You don't have enough supplies to stay," and I told them, "We're good. My guys are good. I've inspected them, and they've got plenty of water and plenty of chow." When you don't move all day, you don't burn a lot of fuel. And you don't use a lot of water when you're in that type of position. You're in the dark all day, in the shade. You're on this concrete floor that's very dirty, but it's cool. I think I brought three big bottles of water in my assault pack for this mission. I ended up drinking only one bottle.

When we finally got pulled out of the hide and got back to Olson, we were all dirty, and the sniper and spotter were still with us. Everybody wanted to know what we saw. We were brought into a briefing room inside the casino, which was nothing more than a quiet area where we could talk with the commander and all the high leadership from the other platoons, because they wanted to know what we saw, what we learned from it. It was basically a way for us to talk about what went wrong, what went right, and how we could make it better next time. Everything you do in the military, you do an after-action review. *Everything.* It's a way for us to constantly improve.

I let them know that I thought we should have been able to shoot and said I didn't like that we had to ask permission, and that it was very hard to communicate. I knew those guys were bad. I was a little passionate, and one of the higher-ups put me in my place, told me to pipe down. Their reasoning for not okaying was that Iraqi policemen were walking around the mosque. But I explained that it had been clear to me that these guys were too far away from the mosque to be police, they were not in uniform, and they hid every time coalition forces flew over. They were not the good guys. Someone said, "We would have liked to have known that information at the time." And I countered, "Well, it's kind of hard to whisper from a sniper hide fifty yards away from a guy who's standing in the middle of a quiet city."

Three months later, when my company was moved north and the Third Battalion 187th took over at the casino base, that mosque blew up. As soon as I heard the news, I made the connection: the bag that guy was carrying was probably explosives. They had been carrying them in, bag by bag, for months. The police were corrupt, they could be bought, so it wouldn't be hard to do. I knew we could have foiled the whole plot if allowed. And I guarantee you that if they had let me shoot them, we would have found explosives in that bag, we would have asked permission to go into that mosque, and we would have found all the explosives hidden in the top of the mosque, because there were tons of them. They had been acquiring them for a long time.

I have observed Iraqis through binoculars and through the scope of my rifle for thousands of hours. I never saw anyone do what they were doing. The other guys in the hide with me felt the same way. We felt like, *Don't waste our time. I've been sliding around on the ground for three days, like Anne Frank in World War II.* That's how it feels when you're in those kind of positions. I don't have Germans breathing down my neck, but I could easily get outnumbered and quickly killed. It's that same idea, it's just hard.

That Golden Dome Mosque was a major holy site. We never targeted mosques. In fact, if a guy shot at you from in front of a mosque, the first thing you would do is shoot back. But if he went inside the mosque, it was over. You'd have to radio back to your lieutenant, who would radio to a captain, who would radio to a battalion commander, who would have to radio all the way to a brigade commander, then to a full-blown colonel to get permission to even touch a mosque. By the time you got that kind of permission, the guy who shot at you would be gone. So the enemy used our rules against us all the time.

The mosque was beautiful, but it was also a divisive point between Muslim groups. There was a lot of animosity between them, so when it blew, it launched a civil war in Iraq.

When I was at Walter Reed, I told people that story. I even told it to the secretary of the Army, who would never get the truth from a battlefield staff sergeant in his day, since they always sugarcoated their reports.

When I returned from Iraq, I sometimes regretted the people I wasn't able to kill only because I knew they were still blowing up citizens and killing our guys. At times, I felt like my hands were tied behind my back because we were always trying to be so politically correct. It wasn't my commanders who made these kinds of rules. They were under such scrutiny from their leadership, who were under such scrutiny from their leadership, who were under such scrutiny from politicians and the media. The war wasn't popular, so we were trying our best not to stir things up.

Still, I knew in my gut those men by the mosque were our enemies. In any other war, they would have been dead. But I was prevented from doing what I thought needed to be done, and I was really upset. I was frustrated, but it didn't stop me. I still went on every sniper mission I was allowed to go on.

Some people have the wrong idea about war. When they hear you've been in combat, they want to know how many bad guys you've killed. They say things like, "You must have been shooting them every day like fish in a barrel." I tell them, "No, not really." Iraqis knew that if they stood and fought with us toe-to-toe, the whole thing would be over in a matter of minutes and we would win. We probably wouldn't lose anybody that way. Their only chance to take us out in numbers was to do IEDs once in a while. That was their only shot. A lot of guys thought it was cowardly, but hey, what's the difference between an IED and dropping a bomb fifty thousand feet that lands in your living room and is now your coffee table? I agree I'd rather have them come out and fight me because I'm infantry and that's how I've trained, but I know they're not stupid. Still, it was pretty frustrating.

I've heard war stories from others who worked in places where they were a little more aggressive and able to kill more of the enemy. I can promise you the areas where we were, we would always put on a very strong front. That was instilled in us by our Rakkasan brigade commander, Colonel Mike Steele. He would tell you, "I want you to look like the meanest son of a bitch when you're riding in that turret through the cities." Don't look at somebody and flinch. Look like an absolute killer, and they won't mess with you. You need to look like a shark everywhere you go. We did that, and sure enough, it worked. We did not get hit as much as other units, even though we still had our share.

CHAPTER 17

Premonitions

Throughout the tour, we alternated sending guys home to the US for a two-week break. I went last, in March 2006, and left Erik Roberts in charge. While I was home, a lot of my friends kept telling me they had a bad feeling, they didn't want me to go back. Of course, everybody's got a bad feeling, I mean, you're going back to war. I told them, "Hey, I'll be all right." I was going to be tough, I was going to be strong. Even though deep down I felt the same way.

I received a call one day before departure, saying, "Hey, your reconnaissance team has moved to Baghdad, so that's where you'll be going when you return." I remembered those areas from back in '03. *Dammit.* "Where in Baghdad?" They told me Sadr City. I couldn't believe it.

Sadr City is the crap hole of Baghdad. It's a perfect square, it's only about a couple miles wide, but there were about two million people in it. They were going to send our company, about a hundred of us, to patrol it. When I reported to the operating base after arrival, my men had already been doing daily patrols in Sadr City for two weeks. I wanted to know what they'd seen. I peppered them with questions: "What's going on? What are the ways in? What are the ways out? What's happened so far?"

They told me, "Every time we go in, we get shot at."

I said, "Okay. What do you do about it?"

They replied, "Some general always gets on the mic from the green zone and tells us to pull out."

So my first patrol in Sadr, true to my men's reports, we got shot at. We were accompanied by the Iraqi Army, friendlies, and I noticed they weren't shooting back. I asked about it and was told they weren't allowed to return fire because they didn't have enough extra rounds. *They don't have enough ammunition?* The next time the enemy started lighting us up, I was like, "Hell with this. Stop the trucks. Let's let them have everything we've got." That was my disgruntled way of saying, "I don't want to be here; Baghdadis don't want me here." It wasn't the right thing to do, according to the leadership, but every time they shot at us, I wanted them to know that we weren't going to run. I felt like they kept getting this sense of confidence, knowing that we would run. I thought that was terrible.

* * *

About two weeks after I returned from my leave, I was approaching 580 days of combat duty. I was a staff sergeant, so I finally had rank to go with the job I'd been doing for more than a year. We only had five months to go on the tour, so I was focusing on the future. My younger brother and I were talking about starting a pool business. I planned to move back to Palm City, get a job as a firefighter, and build pools on the side. Once Kristine graduated from college, we could get married. Positive thoughts like those keep a soldier going during the tough times.

It was April 24, 2006, the anniversary of Troy Jenkins's death. Ever since he was blown up, that day had been bad for me. I didn't want to be around people, I drank too much. I didn't really know how to deal with it. I couldn't talk to anybody about it because none of my buddies had been there. And the guys who were there were wounded and had moved on.

We were on a crap mission, so this day was shaping up to be just as bad. Our assignment was to guard FBI and CIA agents while they tried to identify mass graves as evidence against Saddam Hussein. Saddam didn't like the Shiites, and Sadr City was Shiite central. He was from the Baath Party and liked the Sunnis. He had murdered many of the Shiites and put them in mass graves, so this mission involved locating the bodies so they could be given a proper Muslim burial. This was not a typical infantry mission, and I had a bad feeling about it. This was not a reconnaissance mission, but you don't ask questions. So we were in a dump, and we were digging through trash trying to find bodies. The little kids were running up and throwing bricks at us. There was nothing you could do—we're not going to shoot kids.

Later that evening, back at the base, we were told we needed to go back into the city and recover this truck that had been doing all the digging. I told the lieutenant, "Hey, sir, this is not us. We've never done anything like this. Please send somebody else." He said, "Sergeant, this is something we've got to do."

"Lieutenant, would you just sit down for a second?" I finally told it to him straight. I explained to him the meaning of that day, that Troy had died three years earlier. I told him how it affected me, and he listened, then said, "We've got to go anyway." That was it. I resigned myself. *Okay, we're going.*

It was close to midnight by the time we recovered the truck, but after working twenty-three hours straight without sleep, that day never ended for me. Our convoy was on the way out of the city on a road called Route Predator. That's when I saw the flash, and that's when my world changed. The bomb that detonated was an explosively formed penetrating IED, and it was made in Iran. This particular version was almost always catastrophic. They cost about fifty thousand dollars, and since they were made by Shiites, they were only in Shiite areas.

After the blast and my realization that I'd lost at least one leg, I saw my driver, Shane Irwin, trying to put the vehicle in park because the brakes weren't working. The round that went through me had lodged in the transmission. Military Humvees are really wide, not like the civilian ones. There's probably six feet from the driver to passenger side, plus there's all kinds of gear in between. So even though I was screaming, "Crash the truck! Crash the truck!" Irwin couldn't hear me. The fire was blazing behind our seats, and we couldn't breathe. I saw him open the door; he wanted to jump. I realized, *If this guy jumps, we are done.* Then Irwin looked around in the vehicle and shut the door; he chose to stay in the fire. I remember thinking, *Thank you, Irwin. Thank you.* I can't imagine what courage it took to stay in a fire and burn up rather than leave his men. When Irwin did finally crash into the wall, the force of the wreck almost knocked me out. I tried opening the door, but the blast had buckled it, and it was also blocked by the wall. I tried shouldering it and managed to knock it off the hinges. It's hard to shove against a door when you don't have legs to push with. When it fell open, I rolled out on my face and crawled what felt like a mile, though it was probably only nine feet. I had lost a lot of blood, my right leg was gone, and my left leg was blown in half, hanging by skin. Irwin was the first one to get to me, and he said he was getting help. I heard the medic, Ian Gallegos, going from guy to guy. He was giving directions to the others to tourniquet, and then he got to me, and I saw him put his knee down and take off his huge backpack with all the medical equipment. That told me triage had started; I was pretty sure I was the worst hit.

"How you doing, Murph?" Gallegos asked.

"I'm fine," I responded.

And he nodded. "Do you need morphine?" I said no. "Good, because I wasn't going to give it to you anyway." He kind of laughed.

Gallegos was cool and didn't show any sign of stress. You can't teach that. Maybe they try in medic training, but putting it into practice is entirely different. One minute Staff Sergeant Murphy is walking and talking fine. The next minute, he's lying there smudged in black with just his femur hanging out on one leg, and the other that's mangled with bones. There's the smell of blood and meat and gunpowder and sulfur from the bomb. It's dark and you're not sure the threat is over. People were not holding it together well at that point; some of the young soldiers were freaking out. But the leaders were doing great, their response was flawless, and here was the medic cracking jokes.

There was no time for IVs, mainly just a tourniquet to get the blood stopped, make sure he's breathing, and get him to the base so you can start pumping blood into him and administer drugs.

As we drove onto the base, I saw the medevac coming down, but our vehicle turned the opposite direction. I thought, *Guys, there's my bird. Why are we going that way?* My mind wasn't one hundred percent sharp. I knew my life was on the line, that golden hour, and I knew I wanted to get on that flight.

They took us to an area I'd never been to in the battalion, it was so far out of my league. And they woke all the other medics up. I never expected to see every doc in the whole battalion in that tent. Doc Tenario, who had worked on Troy Jenkins, was working on me. They were checking tourniquets, getting IVs started, getting our paperwork together. We ended up being the worst our company would see the whole deployment.

A lot could still go wrong, and it almost did. They got us to the bird, and since I was the worst injured, they put me on last. The medevac Black Hawk choppers are painted green with a red cross on the side, and they're not set up for carrying troops, only stretchers. Besides the pilot, you have a crew chief who also serves as the in-flight medic and the gunner. He's wearing a flight suit and headset and has a machine gun hanging outside. With the long cable attached to the headset, he can barely get around and check on the patients being transported. It took him a minute or two to get all of us strapped down. In case the pilot had to do some evasive stuff, like avoid an RPG or something, they didn't want us to go slamming into a wall.

The gunner put the oxygen mask on me but didn't turn on the air. I was lying there doing this fish face, sucking plastic. My arms were strapped down, so I couldn't do anything. And the choppers are so loud; he'd never hear me anyway. As I breathed in mask, all I could think was, *You bastard, turn on the air!* The chopper lifted off, and I knew I was going to pass out soon. He finally looked back at me, and his eyes lit up when he realized his error. He started the oxygen, and I was too weak to protest. He almost killed me—I'm not exaggerating. Still angry about that one.

CHAPTER 18
What We Remember

Most wounded service members who get blown up and have catastrophic injuries don't remember the blast. It's mostly adrenalin that gets you through the initial part and shock that makes you forget. I've met at least three hundred guys who have lost limbs. At Walter Reed, I knew about a hundred of them pretty well, plus I've done so many Wounded Warrior Project events and met a few hundred more. But only a handful remember the detail that I can recall. Most said the last thing they remembered was the flash, and then they woke up at Walter Reed. They don't remember being at Landstuhl in Germany at all. It's just really rare for anyone to remember the whole story. They'll say something like, "I remember a doc standing over me and telling me my legs were gone, and then I passed out from the pain." But they remember nothing about the blast itself.

* * *

At Baghdad ER, the tents they took me to after the blast, they asked me if I wanted to call home, and I told them no, I was doing fine. I wasn't up to calling. The medics were kind of insistent: "Do it for your mom or whoever cares about you. You may not make it. We're not saying you're going to die, but people die from these kinds of wounds all the time." *Well, when you put it that way…*

Telephones are not common in combat; infantry guys like me don't carry around cell phones. But this was a place with a bunch of doctors and nurses, so they handed me a satellite phone.

I called my mom first, and I could sense her panic. I couldn't talk very well because my lungs were badly burned and my esophagus was singed, but I told her that there had been an incident and they were going to keep me for a few days. She asked me why my voice was so raspy, and I told her it was because of smoke inhalation. I did not say anything about almost dying or losing my leg. I kept it short and said I would call her when I could.

I called my girlfriend next and told her the same story but added that I'd scratched up my leg. It was challenging to even get that much out. I couldn't talk well while trying to hold myself together. Kristine got off the phone and was crying. Her friend asked, "What did he say?" She told her, "That he scratched his leg." Her friend said, "That doesn't sound so bad," but Kristine said, "You don't know him. He lost his leg. I guarantee it." I fooled my mom, but I didn't fool Kristine.

Before I left on my second tour, I actually asked Kristine, if I lost my arm or leg, would she still love me? She said, "Of course." I had given the possibility some thought, but you can never predict how a catastrophic injury will change things.

After talking to Kristine, I called a couple buddies, and I told them what happened. By that time, I didn't care, so I gave them the full story. They were guys, and I figured they could handle it. I don't know what I expected, but they started friggin' crying. Grown men. You're just never prepared.

I felt the need to be really strong even when I wasn't feeling strong. I felt like crying, but I would never let any of my friends, parents, or their friends think that I wasn't going to be just fine. It's kind of a stupid ego thing. Even if you're not raised to think that "boys don't cry," it's just in you. The older I've gotten, the less it means to keep up that front. I'll cry now, I don't care. But it's still uncomfortable when people see me in a vulnerable position.

The Army had to ask my permission to contact family about my condition, and I said no, absolutely not. I signed something saying that they couldn't. Unfortunately, it didn't work. Mom received a call the next day from the Army saying they needed to go over the extent of her son's injuries, the amputation of the right leg. She told them they'd made a terrible mistake, they were calling the wrong mother— her son was fine, she had talked to me. They finally convinced her it was real and said if she had a passport, the government would help her get to Germany.

* * *

When I woke up at Landstuhl, I was confused. I was on a ventilator in the intensive care unit. I communicated to the nurses by blinking once for yes and twice for no. They kept me sedated for a few days and finally took me off the ventilator. My bed was raised slightly one day, and I saw a doctor come in. He stood over me in his white coat, very businesslike, and told me I'd lost my leg. I said I already knew. Then he said that my left leg was there, but barely. I said I knew that, too.

Then he let me know why he was there. "I need to take your left leg off, and let me tell you why. You're missing nine inches of your calf. You have a compound fracture, your tibia and your fibula. It's a very bad break. We can definitely reattach this, and I bet I can get this leg to live, but you have no idea how bad it's going to be. I won't know if that foot's going to get cold and need to be taken off someday. I don't know if it's going to work. I can tell you right now it's going to be very painful. It's my recommendation that we take it off right at the break, about halfway between your knee and your foot. I think you'll be up and walking a lot faster."

I shifted a little in my bed. The doc handed me a clipboard and pointed. "I just need you to sign right there." He paused and looked at me. "I'll give you some time to think about it. I know this is really hard, but we think it's better for you. Just trust me." Then he left.

This was a difficult decision to make, one that would impact the rest of my life. I was still pretty out of it, and I didn't have anybody to advise me—my family was thousands of miles away. I didn't have anyone to call. My mother was inconsolable, and they still hadn't located my dad so he didn't even know about the blast.

As I lay there thinking about signing the form, a nurse came in. She said, "You don't have to do this."

I looked at her. "What do you mean?" I was thinking, *Who are you? Are you like that creepy flight attendant? The doctor said to do it. I'm in the Army. I do what I'm told.*

She said, "You have another option. It's called limb salvage."

I wasn't buying it. "He just told me that's very painful and it would probably need to be taken off someday anyway."

She looked straight at me. "Yeah, but you never know unless you try. There's a chance that your leg will be—not perfect—but good enough. Think about it." And she left.

The doc came in a few minutes later, and I told him, "I think I'm going to give it a shot—limb salvage. Is that an option?" His face dropped, and he started looking around. I realized I probably screwed up by using the medical term, limb salvage. He took the clipboard and form, then looked right at me. "If you weren't awake right now, I'd take your leg anyway, because I wouldn't need your consent." It wasn't like he was being a jerk, he was telling me like it is. "This is the best for you. I'm a doctor. Whoever told you that is a nurse." His point: nurses don't cut on people.

The doctor left the room, and I heard him yelling at somebody and figured it was the nurse. Of course, he was one hundred percent right. He was right on everything, every detail: the difficulty of saving the leg, the pain of rehabilitation. But I didn't sign that form, and I've still got my leg today thanks to that nurse.

And I can tell you there were so many times at Walter Reed I wished I had listened to him. It hurt so bad. All my double-amputee buddies were up walking and smiling after a few months, and their families were clapping. Meanwhile, I was lying over there in a corner not even allowed to stand yet because the bones weren't strong enough. I kept thinking, *What did I do?* I saw other guys in limb salvage who had been there two years. They were pale and suffering every day in pain. And most of them eventually had their leg chopped off, like he said. I'm one of the few still rocking it.

I don't think people can really relate to the kind of pain we're talking about, which affects you on a daily basis. I guess you can imagine shooting somebody in the leg with a shotgun hundreds of times, and that's kind of what it's like. Your leg is there, but it's a constant source of pain. So I don't know if it was the right decision, but I tell you, I don't like putting a fake leg on the stump every day, either. The process is not fun.

Putting it on in the morning is miserable. You know, I've been in a warm bed, my stump is warm, and I have to grab the cold liner and slide it painfully over the warm body part. It doesn't feel good. Then I go to put the leg on and try to stand up and start pushing. There have been times that I've started walking out to get the coffee going and looked down and realized the right foot is toed out, the toe is pointing the wrong way, so I have to sit down, take it off, and readjust. There's always discomfort. Every day is different, and some days are better than others. If I had two fake legs, then I'd have two fitting issues; maybe two legs would be toed out and I'd be walking like a duck.

Then again, the docs told me if I had two fake legs, I could run, and I can't run now, so I don't know. There are all kinds of trade-offs, I guess.

After they transferred me to a regular room at Landstuhl, someone from the medical team said they were going to do a washout the following day. I asked what that meant. "You're going to be on a stretcher, naked, and they're going to irrigate your wounds with saline to decrease bacteria." I thought, *That doesn't sound very bad; whatever they need to do.* I woke up after that procedure and was in worse pain than directly after the blast. I thought, *Oh my god, what in the world?* My jaw was bruised, my face hurt. Every muscle in my arms hurt. *What did they do, squirt me with a pressure washer? I mean, I'm blown up!*

They gave me a day off, but said I would have to go back for another washout the following day. And they kept repeating the procedure. Every time I came out of a washout, I was in terrible shape. The idea was to try to prevent infection, and maybe it helped prevent some, but I've still had plenty of them over the years.

When you're riding in a Humvee through a desert or city, there's trash on the ground, dust, and dirt. When a bombs goes off, it just blows all that into you—millions of little pieces. It's not like a surgeon can pick the stuff out. I still have probably fourteen pieces in me that they can't get to. I've pulled out at least twenty pieces including copper from the bomb, metal from the door, and even pieces of my weapon that were inside of me. Some guys have stuff lodged up against their spine. You're not going to go in and mess around near somebody's spine.

The washouts were mainly trying to get out as much junk as possible. But they can squirt forever and not get it all out. A lot of it stays, unfortunately. Still, they were doing the best they could.

I kept wondering, *When are you going to sew up my stump?* Someone finally told me that it would have to wait until I transferred to the States. They were just doing the basic surgeries and the washouts at Landstuhl, and stabilizing my "good" leg. They straightened it, screwed a bolt into my bone above the knee and by my ankle and attached those to a metal bar to stabilize it. It couldn't be set because of all the swelling. I didn't know it at the time (thankfully), but that ended up being major surgery followed by an external fixator—I call it the cage. I had to wear it for nine months. Yeah, that was a bitch.

* * *

One of the nurses mentioned that my guys were at Landstuhl—Sergeant Erik Roberts, my second-in-command and team leader, and Private First Class Adam Jefferson. I asked, "Can I see them?" They said they would try to bring them to my room, since I couldn't be moved. Roberts had a massive laceration on his right leg and a compound fracture of the femur. Jefferson had a compound fracture, too, and both had devices holding their legs together. But my injuries were more severe. A few minutes later, I was surprised to see nurses wheeling the guys' beds into my hospital room, with all their medical tubing and wiring. It was so cramped, there was no space for anyone to walk between us. It was great to be with them again. We joked around and talked about what we remembered. It was funny, because each of us recalled parts of that day that the others didn't.

One thing I noticed was how much our personalities had changed. It was as if we weren't really in the military anymore. We absolutely were, of course, but all the rules and regulations were gone, the hierarchy broken down. We were just buddies; the injuries had somehow leveled us.

I remember Roberts smiling. He was just so happy that he was alive. That kid prayed so hard for hours the night of the blast, whereas I, who went to church my entire life—probably more than he did—I was talking to *me*. Like, *Stay in it. Stay in it. Stay awake. Stay awake.* I didn't feel like I had time to pray. I remember thinking it was good that Roberts was praying, but also thinking, *I've got to pump myself up.* It was all I could do. I felt like if I turned it over to God, I would be gone. I mean seriously. Sure, God was there, and he was helping, but Roberts was praying and I wasn't, and it didn't bother me.

Now that we were at Landstuhl Medical, Roberts kept smiling. Of course, he was in pain, but we were all really happy to be alive. We were all extremely pale, since we'd lost so much blood. I also kept remembering that this was where Sergeant Troy Jenkins died—Landstuhl. He had been brought there like me and like them. But he didn't make it home.

They brought the guys to see me three times, but not in a row because I was having to go through those friggin' washouts. Even as bad as I felt, I looked forward to those visits. It was a connection I needed as I faced the uncertainties of the future, the unfamiliar. They were my guys. And we had this new thing in common: we were Wounded Warriors.

One morning, a lady came in to ask what I wanted for breakfast, and I asked if I could see my guys. She said, "Sorry, they flew out this morning."

I felt like, *What? I didn't authorize that. Nobody told me.* There was this constant reminder: *You're not in charge anymore, dude. You're just a blown-up guy.*

You're not in charge, your guys are gone, and you didn't get to say good-bye. I was a little pissed off and a little sad and kind of worried that I was left behind.

I asked where they went. "They were sent back to the hospital at Fort Campbell. You're going to go to Walter Reed in Washington, DC." I thought, *We're going to separate places?* That didn't sit well. I asked why I was going to Walter Reed, and she said, "You're an amputee." Translation: *You're going to have a long damn road ahead.* I had never heard of Walter Reed Army Medical Center, so I had no idea what to expect.

For that short time, Roberts, Jefferson, and I had been a small force, an awkward force. We were a squad of three. And now, for the first time, I felt really alone. For six and a half years, I had been told where to be and when to be there, and I was part of a squad, part of a platoon, part of a company, a battalion, a brigade, a division. Things were different now. I was now on this personal journey—just me—to see if I could get better.

CHAPTER 19
Blast-Wound Guys

I didn't know what was going to happen to me day to day, and I can't stand not knowing. The nurses are very well trained in what to say. They don't act like anything is really wrong with you. They greeted me, "Hey, how are you doing?" I would reply, "I think I'm good, I guess." They would take care of a few things, then say, "All right! Good! See you later." Everything was upbeat, positive. They would make comments like, "Oh, man, you're going to get a cool leg, you're going to get a running leg." When I asked more in-depth questions, they avoided giving detail, but convinced me everything in my life would be the same. They showed me pictures of guys with a fake leg running. I believed what they said and even repeated it to my family and friends when they called. But these people were not therapists, they didn't know the rehabilitation process. They were just being upbeat and confident and keeping me pumped up, which is the best thing at that point, to be surrounded by positive attitudes.

One of the advantages service members have that other regular amputees don't have is a community in common, at least in the beginning. People who see my injury tell me about relatives who have lost a leg to diabetes. They often talk about the person being depressed because they don't know anyone else who has lost a leg. That might be a way that veterans have it easier. We have a huge support group from the start, people to encourage us, to tell us we're going to run marathons.

At the time, you can still think positively, too. You have no idea how bad it will hurt, and you don't know anything about prosthetics.

You don't know how hard it is to build up the core muscles that it takes to push prostheses. How after being fitted you can only stand about twenty seconds the first time. And forty seconds the next day. A week can go by before you've even taken your first step. You don't know about the recurring surgeries, constant pain, sleepless nights. You don't know what the limitations are going to be—the "new normal." That's when so many veterans lose hope, too.

But early on, when they tell you everything's going to be all right, you have this false sense of security. And it works.

One day at Landstuhl, a woman came into my room and was kind of making small talk. Then she started telling me a story about how Jack and Jill went down the hill and did this and that. And they met Peter. Then they went over the river and did this and that. At the end she said, "Who did they meet?" I said, "Peter." And that, it turned out, was my traumatic brain injury test. The Army now does a baseline on every guy when they enlist. Then, if you get blown up, they'll do another baseline. They started these baselines sometime during my second tour because head trauma had become such an epidemic with the IEDs. At Walter Reed, I saw guys all the time walking around with flash cards, trying to get back what they lost. These guys went from being grown men to not understanding they couldn't fit an entire grocery store into their shopping cart. They were as clueless as their eight-year-old. I'm still friends with a bunch of them, and they are still struggling.

Early on at Landstuhl, I was lying there, and at that point I had not experienced any infections. All my muscles were Jell-O, and I felt like somebody had beaten me with a bat everywhere. A nurse walked in with a clipboard and asked me how I was feeling. I told her, "Fine."

She said, "On a scale of one to ten, with ten being the most unimaginable pain, what's your level?"

I said, "Probably a three."

She gave me a doubtful look. "A three out of one to ten?"

I said, "Yeah, it's been a four a couple times, but probably just a three right now."

She started to mark her pad and said, "What did you do in the military?" I told her I was in the infantry. "Oh," she said, "so it's probably like a seven."

I was pretty irritable from the pain and answered, "Maybe like someone else's nine, but it's not as bad as when they were dragging me down the road, ma'am." I was about to tell her that all her questions were making my pain climb to a three and a half.

Then she asked, "How's your upper-body strength?"

I said, "It's fine. On the upper body, I've got burns. That's what all these bandages are for. But I'm okay."

She told me she needed to test my arm strength. I didn't hesitate. I grabbed the pole above my bed, the one used for transfers, and did three quick pull-ups. My left (good) leg was elevated on a pillow, and my right one was gone, of course, so it was a little bit awkward, but maybe that would give her what she needed.

She smiled, "Okay, okay," and wrote something on the clipboard, then left.

Whatever she wrote was a continued source of entertainment for everyone else reading my chart. One guy looked at it and said, "So you can do pull-ups? Don't do any more pull-ups." It definitely stopped people from asking about my upper-body strength. They'd shake their head and smile when they read the file.

I thought about that incident months later when I was at Walter Reed. I was down to 124 pounds and couldn't do a pull-up even if I wanted to. I could barely get myself out of bed, and I had a constant fever. When I was finally able to move around, I still wasn't strong enough to push my wheelchair when it hit the carpet.

* * *

A below-the-knee amputation is night and day from an above-the-knee, which is what I have on my right leg. We call below-the-knee amputations "paper cuts." Those guys don't like to hear it, but there is a huge difference. It's a matter of joints. Moving a two-joint artificial leg, meaning an artificial knee and ankle, takes about five times more strength than moving a regular leg. And that's with a computerized prosthetic.

There's also a huge difference in how an amputation occurs. For example, if you're riding a motorcycle and you hit a guardrail and your leg goes, that's more surgical compared to a blast wound. Doctors reminded us of our uniqueness all the time. They would say things like, "You blast-wound guys," as if we were an entirely different category. It's the worst possible scenario for a surgeon, I think. If we didn't have the docs dealing with our type of injuries all the time, knowing what to look for, we would be dead. If I had been in Vietnam and not gotten out of the jungle in an hour—that golden hour—I would have been dead. Having medics in the field with us makes a huge difference as well. And medical advances keep improving our odds. I met guys who fought at the latter end of the Vietnam War, who got to keep their legs because of the development of Cipro, an antibiotic used to fight bacterial infections.

War blast victims also throw a curve ball to American medicine because nonmilitary docs don't see the types of complications we have every day. For example, in 2013, I started getting fevers every day plus swelling and redness in my stump. I went in for emergency surgery, and the doc discovered that the end of my bone had rotted, literally. That's what he said: "It's crumbling. It's gooey and nasty." The cause turned out to be bacteria that had been in me since the blast. The antibiotics they'd put me on seven years earlier at Walter Reed hadn't been strong enough to kill it because it was not native to the US. I'd had a rare version of pseudomonas living in my body and never knew it until I started having the fevers and pain. The pseudomonas can get into your bloodstream and kill you. After they took an inch and a half of my femur, I went through weeks of trying different antibiotics until they found one that worked.

* * *

I spent about a week at Landstuhl before going to Walter Reed. I couldn't wait to get out of Germany. I just wanted to be back in the States. I had no idea what was ahead of me and how much the surgeries would suck at Walter Reed, too. All I knew was that what I had experienced so far was not fun. When I arrived at Walter Reed, they knocked me out—they put me in to some sort of an induced coma for about two days of surgeries. When I woke up, my right leg was still not stitched up and they hadn't taken my left leg, either.

I didn't have email, and I didn't have any contact with the outside world at that point. I was just in this bed. I had a little TV that was about six inches by four inches on a white swiveling stand, but it was still really hard for me to focus on the screen. They had me on a lot of drugs. They were also waking me up every thirty minutes to check my heartbeat and blood pressure. So even when I did finally doze off, every thirty minutes I woke up to the sound of a cart and someone announcing, "Vitals!" Then they'd come in and shoot me with a needle and change my IV line every other day. I was seeing a lot of people, but I didn't know anybody. I had not heard from my guys and really didn't know the location or size of Walter Reed.

Someone told me that my family would be coming to see me, so I started planning for it when I was conscious. I was trying to mentally prepare. I thought I was going to cry when I saw them, and I was worried about that. My main worry was being in such a weak state. I was in denial. I was still Staff Sergeant Murphy. I still thought, *I've got to kick your ass.* At the same time, I thought I was very close to death, not out of danger yet. I was stable but had infections cropping up constantly. Docs warn you about the risks of infection with every surgery, and guys like us have twenty or thirty in our first year. A lot of things could go wrong. Blood clots were even scarier than infections. They could go through your lungs and from there to your heart or up to your brain and cause an aneurism or a stroke. I had clots in my lungs, but fortunately they caught them early. There were threats everywhere, and the biggest was the threat of the unknown. It wasn't something we talked a lot about or dwelled on when we lost someone. It was just our world.

I was worried about how to greet my family, rehearsing it in my mind. "How are you doing?" or smiling, giving them a hug. And I knew they were going to friggin' cry all over me. I was worried about how they were going to take it. I was so bad looking, you know? My stump was huge, all swollen and wrapped with gauze. My other leg was wrapped and hooked to a hanging bar to keep it elevated, and I was extremely pale. When I used a hand mirror to shave, I saw how my blue eyes had turned dull and gray. Even when I tried to practice a confident look, I knew it wasn't convincing. Besides that, the burns behind my neck were bandaged, the bandages stuck out above my hospital gown, and there was a catheter bag hanging from the side of the bed. My six-foot frame was becoming bonier by the day. I didn't have an appetite and had difficulty keeping food down because of the drugs. I barely had enough strength to shift my body using the trapeze bar overhead. I was nervous about the first meeting with each person

I met. I was very, very worried about how they would react to seeing me. I wanted to make it easy on them. I almost wanted to put a blanket over myself and slowly show them.

My third day at Walter Reed, I was lying there, and the nurse came in and said, "There's someone here who wants to see you." It was my girlfriend, Kristine. She was the first person from home to arrive. It meant a lot that she was first.

When she walked in, she burst into tears and ran toward me. She slowed when she saw all the medical equipment and realized she couldn't hug me too hard because I was so banged up. I noticed she didn't have on makeup and her hair wasn't done; she had just tried to get there as fast as she could. She told me she left in the middle of college finals week. Kristine was an exercise science major, which is premed and pretty intense. So that was a huge sacrifice. I also knew she didn't have any money and was not the type to go anywhere on her own, but she had made it, driving almost thirteen hours from Tallahassee, Florida, to Bethesda, Maryland, just outside of Washington, DC. This was before smart phones and GPS in our cars. She said she was staying with an aunt and uncle who lived about forty-five minutes away. Still, I was sure she was going broke trying to be there for me, but I wasn't in a position to help her out. It was stressful for both of us.

A few days after Kristine arrived, my mom made it. I asked about Dad and was told nobody knew where he was. He was retired and visiting a friend in Mexico, but obviously not checking his email, and he didn't have a cell phone.

Dad made it about ten days later. He beat himself up over that one. He and mom were both there for a long time, but it got to be too much. They had been divorced a number of years, and the hospital was very tight quarters. When the two of them started bickering, I told Mom it would be best if she went home. She'll tell you, boy, she was not happy. Another hard decision, but it was something I had to do.

CHAPTER 20
The Nurse in Charge

As good as the medical care was at Walter Reed, some of the errors cost me. A nurse put a rubber strap over my foot and attached it to the metal fixator to try to offset drop foot. Three days later, a nurse pulled back the sheet and reacted, "Oh. My. God." Of course, I couldn't see anything, and asked, "What?" I had so much pain everywhere else, I couldn't feel the bedsores that had developed on my heel and the pad of my foot. You can lose parts of your body to bedsores. They eventually healed after six months, but to this day, the most pain I have on a daily basis is the bottom of my foot from those pressure sores.

Right after the bedsore incident, a nurse was trying to move me from a potty chair back into the hospital bed, and I ended up on the ground. The fall yanked my leg and I yelled in pain. My eleven-inch laceration on the good leg busted open and hit the ground, where all the staph germs are. The docs told me they would have to do emergency surgery to fix it. All I could think was, *Oh, I don't want another surgery...I don't want a staph infection. Why me?*

There were some experimental procedures that didn't go well, either, at least initially. The docs told me they could place a filler where my gastrocnemius (calf muscle) used to be. It was made up of bovine (cow) tissue. I went in for surgery, and they sewed the flesh into me. I woke up the next day and it hurt like hell. They said they'd watch it for twenty-four hours. The next day I saw the doctor's face when he checked it. I could only see their faces, I couldn't see what was going on down there, and I didn't like the face he was making, so I said, "What's the problem?" He said, "I'm not sure yet. It's still too early to tell, but it doesn't look like it's happy. It doesn't look like it took." He said they'd give it another day. I started to get a fever and found out that the thing was basically starting to rot inside of me. It wouldn't friggin' live. I asked, "What does this mean?" They said they were going to have to take it out.

"Like, surgery?"

"Oh, yeah."

"And then you're going to try again with another surgery?"

"Yeah."

"When?"

"Probably tomorrow. I'll try to get you in early, but you know, maybe around two." So there would be the presurgery prep, nothing to eat or drink after midnight. I was taking all these drugs on an empty stomach; it was pure torture. Starving, pain, meds on an empty stomach, then surgery. What a life.

After the next surgery, when they installed all the new flesh and closed me up, ninety percent of it took. They were happy with that amount. Next was a skin graft. They cheese-grated some skin off my thigh and stitched it up. The skin was used to close a nine-inch hole on my calf, over the bovine tissue. To help the thigh area heal, they put a thin layer of phyllo-looking cloth and goo on it. They added layer after layer on about sixteen inches of my leg. When I became conscious again, it was burning and oozing, and I was in intense pain. The best way I can describe it is if someone took a hot iron and stuck it on your thigh, pulled it off, and did it again. All of this on top of all my "normal" pain. They brought a lamp in that took the burn away, and I would alternate from heat and no pain to chills and intense pain.

Besides the twenty months I spent on deployment, every day felt like an eternity at that point in my recovery. For week and weeks, the thigh wound got crusty and pieces would peel off. People coming to visit would see the rust-looking stuff and try to clean it off the sheets, thinking the nurses weren't caring for me. But it was constant, you couldn't keep the sheets clean.

It was just a miserable, humiliating, vulnerable, embarrassing, not-cool experience. And I had to still try to be tough, obviously. You don't want anybody to think you're a wimp.

All of this started getting to me, and I got a little excessive on the nurse call button. There were a lot of us service members there, so you couldn't dominate the nurse. With all the pain and procedures, though, I must have been angry and sarcastic when someone from the nurse station answered. A few minutes later, this woman came in. She was probably forty years old and had some years in the business. She loaded me into a wheelchair and started rolling me down the hall. All of a sudden, she took a sharp left into a room where they store all the linens. I had never been in that room, and it was quiet. No one else was in there. The nurse locked the door and came to the front of my chair and said, "You listen here and you listen good. I have a lot of you guys in here. We don't have time for that kind of attitude or language."

I looked up at her and could tell she meant business. I said, "Yes, ma'am."

She walked around the back of my chair, opened the door, and backed me out of there like all was well.

I swear to God, I never acted up again. She set me straight. I tell you what, it had a good effect on me.

* * *

I'm from a small community in South Florida, and when word got around that I was injured, some people got together and started talking

Top: I bought my first truck, a Ford F-150, before I was licensed to drive. My friend Eric Heizler had a Chevy.

Center: Toward the end of my first deployment, we were near Tal Afar in northern Iraq. There are pads on the cots, which is about the best we ever had it. That 4x8 area made up my entire "personal" living space, a far cry from sleeping in trash on the streets of Baghdad.

Bottom: This was late in 2005 in Samarra, right around the time of the Blue Door Alley sniper hide and prior to the Golden Mosque getting blown up. I was on watch in the OP4.

Top: Before deployment, you've trained so hard physically and mentally, you're just ready to get it started. This is our third platoon just before departure to Iraq in September of 2005.

Center Left: I'm patrolling in Sadr City just a few weeks before the IED destroyed our Humvee. I had just been promoted to Staff Sergeant and it looks like I'm expecting trouble. (Photo by Erik Roberts)

Center Right: Also in Sadr City. A car bomb had killed and wounded dozens of civilians. The photographer in the background beat us to the blast; he was clearly tipped off.

Bottom: Shane Irwin, on the right, was driving the Humvee when we were blown up, two days after this photo was taken. We were in Sadr City, one of the most dangerous places to be patrolling on foot.

Above: February 25, 2006,
what my weapon looked like
before it was blown in half.
That Colt M4Carbine was my
baby. A short version of the
M16, it had a custom handle,
an ACOG scope and TAC 2
infrared laser. In a quarter of
a second, I could have that
thing pointed and shooting.
You always had to be ready.
(Photo by Erik Roberts)

Top: April 25, 2006 – my
"Alive Day."

Bottom: I took my first few
steps about four months after
the blast. It was a pretty big
deal. My mom, Willi Murphy,
is helping, and my first therapist at Walter Reed, Cari, is
standing in the background.

Top: We were back at Fort Campbell in February or March of 2004 and everyone had a CIB. On the left is Brian Buss and on the right is George Faulk and we are part of the Third Battalion, 187th Infantry Regiment, also known as the Iron Rakkasans.

Bottom: When my friends put together a fundraiser to help offset costs for family to visit me at Walter Reed, John Pierson made a significant donation. He's pictured here with my mom, Willi, at the July 1, 2006 barbecue.

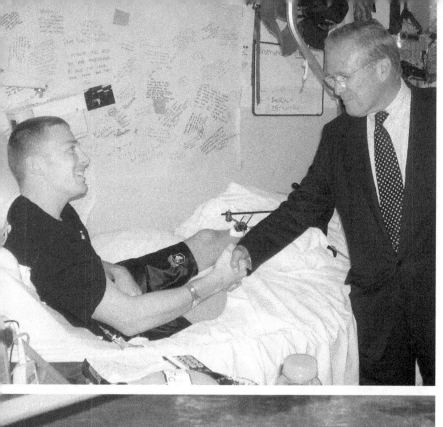

Opposite Page:

Top: Former Secretary of Defense Donald Rumsfeld was one of my early visitors during my year at Walter Reed. We had celebrities, politicians, and even the president drop in, often visiting us in our rooms.

Bottom: This swimming pool therapy was not on the approved activities list, but it sure felt good after months of surgeries, chronic pain and generally just feeling lousy.

This Page:

Top:This was about four months after the blast and the first time I'd seen my fellow wounded warriors, Erik Roberts (left) and Adam "AJ" Jefferson, since our hospital stay in Germany.

Bottom: Cher was part of my parents' generation, but even I recognized her when she visited Walter Reed.

Top: Against my doctors' advice, I flew to Ft. Campbell to greet the guys when they returned from deployment. I was dizzy and nauseous and still had problems with my "good" leg, the one in the external fixator (the cage). There were other obstacles, but I made it. What a great moment.

Center: Mary Bryant McCourt is founder of Achilles Freedom Team of Wounded Veterans and she brought her still-on-stage smile to Walter Reed along with some adaptive bikes for us to try. One ride and I was hooked.

Bottom: A lot of organizations sponsor trips to help wounded warriors. The Telluride Adaptive Sports Program brought a group of us out to Colorado. On this particular climb, I'm about 70 feet up.

Above: The Achilles Freedom Team of Wounded Veterans traveled to Rio de Janeiro, Brazil, where I took second place. Racing helped me realize I wasn't handicapped at all. I'm still competing, still sweating. I'm still in the game.

Above: One of my first major
mentors, John Pierson, had an
Army helicopter brought in for
one o f his parties when they
designated April 25th "Luke
Murphy Day" in Martin
County.

Above: My visits to sites from other wars have helped put my injury and sacrifice in perspective. Every battle has something to teach us.

Top: A last minute invitation won a spot for me on Jimmy Buffet's boat, the Last Mango. I caught a yellowfin that day, unusual without a trip "across" to the Bahamas.

Center: Stephanie and I had similar tastes in music and the outdoors, and when I got to know her first as a friend, I thought she was a pretty complete girl. I still can't find any flaws.

Bottom: On a three-day Soldier Ride from Miami to Key West even though we weren't racing, I still liked being in the lead.

Top: While overseas, we took some time to visit the medical staff at Landstuhl. The ICU staff see the worst injuries and rarely hear what happens after the service members leave. I wanted them to know what a guy looks like when he's finally upright again.

Center: My "second" photo with Mr. Trump...

Bottom: Colonel Steele invited me to Atlanta in 2009 for a "Faces of Freedom" fundraiser Skeet Shoot. I met former Georgia Bulldogs Coach Vince Dooley, who Steele played for in college. He still looked like he could beat somebody up.

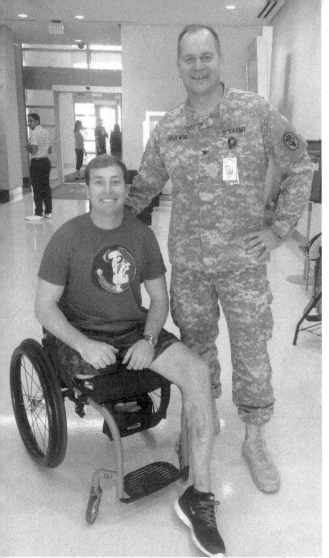

This Page:
In 2014, Dr. Donald Gajewski ("Guyeski"), who did my original surgery at Walter Reed, performed my 32nd surgery at the Center for the Intrepid at the San Antonio Military Medical Center. He's considered the "Michelangelo of Amputees.".

Opposite Page:
Top: On my left is Bobby Jindal, governor of Louisiana, and on my right is Florida Governor Rick Scott. They were presenting me with a Spirit of Service award in 2014 for my work with veterans and the community.

Bottom: Since my first experience on a mono ski with the National Disabled Veterans Winter Sports Clinic while still a patient at Walter Reed I've skied black diamonds and almost killed myself on a mono ski. Maybe it's a good thing I'm marrying an ICU nurse. She likes to ski, too.

Above: That's my nephew, Dylan Jr., on my shoulders; my brother, Aran; Willi, my mother; Larry, my father; nephew Logan; my brother, Dylan Sr., and our oldest brother, Eddie.

about ways to help. The parents of my good friends knew my family was having trouble paying for expenses to visit. The government pays for immediate family to travel once or twice, but I have three brothers, and they all wanted to come. These days there are all kinds of nonprofits that gladly help—like the Wounded Warrior Project. But in 2006, Wounded Warriors was a really small organization. At the time, there was a Yellow Ribbon Fund, which provided guys rental cars for their families, but that group had a tight budget as well.

Two of my friends called my mom and said they wanted to put on a fundraising benefit for me. My mom came to my hospital room and told me about the idea. I immediately said, "No way. I don't want anybody doing anything like that for me. I'm fine." I just didn't want anybody going out of their way. I'd never heard of anyone doing that for my peers at Walter Reed, and I felt embarrassed about it. So she said okay and told them.

My friends called me direct and said, "Listen, you little punk," and eventually got me on board. They told me some of the people behind it, parents of my friends mostly, and I knew I was going to lose anyway. They're very convincing. I started thinking that a get-together might be a way for my family and friends to cope with my injury. And it might be a way to help my family get back and forth to visit me. But never in my wildest dreams did I think it would draw as many people as it did.

The local news sent a reporter up to Walter Reed, and he wrote a story before the event. It seemed that every organization I had ever been a part of wanted to help. Paul Filipe, who owns a big landscape company in Palm City, has a large spread out west of town with soccer fields, so he could accommodate the crowds. I had never met this man, but some of his very close friends knew me, so he agreed to host it.

Some people told my friends they were crazy and wouldn't be able to raise much money, but they went forward with it. I received phone calls and messages saying, "We hope to see you at the event." I'm like, *Really? I can't even leave this hospital room, and you want me to come to Florida? Come see my buddies?* Of course I wanted to see everybody, but it wasn't possible. The event was planned for Saturday, July 1, 2006, a little over eight weeks after my injury. I was not in good shape.

The organizers presold ten-dollar tickets, and over a thousand people went. There was barbecue and beer. They cooked nine pigs over a smoker and more than three hundred chickens. Some people were making other donations and buying T-shirts with the 101st Airborne insignia that said, *Benefit for Staff Sergeant Luke Murphy.* My buddies volunteered their time, and that was a big deal for them. Some of my schoolteachers came, and the things they told the reporter made me wonder if they had me confused with someone else. *Sweet? Helpful? Wait a minute, you're the teacher who wrote me up! I probably gave you gray hair.* It's just funny that people remember only the good things about you when you're lying there half-dead.

Guys from the ranch where I had worked in high school brought their kids, and someone sent me a photo of my younger brother doing an interview with the TV news. I thought, *Oh, man, poor Dylan.* He had never been in front of a camera before, and here he was a celebrity. I know how awkward it feels. Even though I couldn't be there, I really appreciated everything that my town did.

An event closer to the hospital that I thought I might be able to make was the Fourth of July celebration on the West Lawn of the US Capitol in DC. When I first heard about it only a few weeks after my arrival at Walter Reed, I thought it sounded like a zoo and didn't want to go. But the rehab techs said we definitely should go because we would get a shout-out from the president and would be in a VIP section at the front.

Achieving that goal would be huge for me because of what it would require physically. The plan was for me to meet with other wounded service members after lunch on July 4 at Walter Reed. We would be loaded on a bus, which takes forever, since they have to use a lift for each person. Then they would have to secure every wheelchair with buckles on the floorboard. Even though it was a short drive, with the Washington, DC, traffic, it might take an hour and a half. They would unload us, then take us to a staging area. And because it's a military event, we'd have to be there at least an hour early. It would be an all-day affair followed by fireworks exploding over the Washington Monument. We wouldn't be home until midnight.

I had to weigh all these steps carefully. I wanted to go, but I also knew that if I even hit a crack on the sidewalk, my bones rattled and it hurt. The few times I had ridden in the back of a bus for hospital-arranged dinners, even for twenty minutes, I got nauseous. But it was a goal for me and for the staff trying to get me there, trying to get me well enough to go.

I didn't make it. I heard everybody leaving that day, but I stayed behind because I felt like hell and had a fever, which turned out to be an infection. Guys who were hurt after my injury were going, but I realized you can't compare yourself to others. Everybody heals at a different rate. Sometimes you set a goal and your body doesn't cooperate—there's nothing you can do. I could hear the celebration from my room, and I wished I could have gone. But at the end of the day, I knew it was the right decision. I figured it was better to be miserable at Walter Reed than on the West Lawn in full view of everyone, in constant pain as well as miserable. It was just another setback. Time to move on to the next goal.

CHAPTER 21

Comeback

In the fall of 2006, about six months after my injury, the nurses and the occupational and physical therapists started talking about a visitor who was coming to Walter Reed. He ran a program to take wounded veterans skiing in Aspen, Colorado. They provided all the adaptive gear on the slopes, and when the wounded guys came back from the trip, they always said it was a blast. He was supposed to be coming in two weeks. "Make sure you're at occupational therapy at two—you don't want to miss it."

About a week out, I kept hearing, "Hey, don't forget. Winter Sports Clinic is coming to talk. They'll show a video. It's really funny. Make sure you're there." They said the trip wouldn't be until the spring of the following year, so we had time to get better, but they didn't want us to miss the meeting. I thought, *Okay, okay. We're there.* My dad was retired and had moved to DC to help in my rehabilitation. So when the day came, he reminded me, "Don't forget the ski-trip meeting." Okay, I *got* it. In physical therapy that morning, I heard it repeated, "Don't forget about this!" Geez. So I wheeled my chair into OT that afternoon, and all my buddies were there, at least the ones who were interested. There were probably forty of us wounded guys, plus parents, girlfriends, and wives. There were little kids running around, and all our OT and PT therapists were standing in the back.

A fiftyish athletic-looking guy with dark hair and a bushy mustache was visiting with some of the therapists and then moved to the front. He was wearing a long-sleeved shirt and vest, like he was dressed for the

slopes. "I'm Sandy Trombetta, and I want to take every one of you skiing in Snowmass next spring—if you're willing to go." I looked around
the room. Some of these guys had one leg and no other limbs. Guys
were missing essential parts of their body—maybe a hand or fingers.
Most of us were in wheelchairs, and I thought, *Dude, you're friggin' nuts.*

He was very convincing. "I don't care if you've got arms or legs. If
you've got some kind of muscle, any kind of muscle, you can do it." He
said it was up to us to train for the trip. "I need you to train whatever
muscle you've got left. If you've only got abs, then train those. You do
your part, and I promise I'll do my part. I'll get you skiing." I was still
pretty doubtful, until I actually saw guys like us on his video. There
were blind guys skiing, above-the-knee double amputees, men with
no arms. They were all bundled up in ski masks and jackets, and had
snow sprayed across their faces. They were crashing into snowdrifts
and coming up laughing. That did it for me.

Trombetta told us a little about himself. He was the founder of the
National Disabled Veterans Winter Sports Clinic, which is sponsored
by the Department of Veterans Affairs and funded by businesses and
individuals who donate money and services. What he was offering was
basically an all-expense paid vacation. I knew I wanted to go. But I still
had that darn cage on my good leg, so that became my goal, to get it
taken off so I could go skiing.

The way I looked at it, this was just another place the Army
wanted to send me. I was still in the military. It's not like I was free
to go off on my own, to go anywhere that wasn't within the military's
plan for my life. I might have left the streets of Iraq, but I was still a
soldier. For six years, I went where I was told, when I was told, and
lived mostly outside of the civilian world. I had taken one short trip
to Florida accompanied by my dad as part of the transition, but it
had been very difficult. This time I was going on my own, without

my dad or girlfriend there to help. I knew it would be a significant accomplishment.

A few months before the trip, it was looking like I wasn't going to make it. The doctor who put the external fixator (the cage) on my leg said I wasn't ready. I kept begging him to take it off so I'd have time to heal, but he wasn't budging. Finally, two weeks before the trip, another doctor came to my defense. I had known Dr. Donald Gajewski (pronounced "Guyeski") from my first days at Walter Reed, and he asked the cage doc point blank: "Why not?" The doc said my good leg wasn't strong enough to be used without the cage, even though I promised him, "I'll be good." Dr. G helped me out by doing the surgery himself. He knew me better than anyone at that hospital, and he had performed a lot of surgeries on me already. One of the things he knew was that I wasn't easy to knock out. When he walked into the operating room, I was still making wisecracks, so he told the anesthesiologist, "Hit him again." But they couldn't, he'd already given me a horse load. Dr. G went ahead and unscrewed the pins from my bones, released me from the cage, and bandaged the leg. I remember everything.

April 5, 2007, less than a year after the blast, about fourteen of us limbless guys in wheelchairs, on crutches, and with empty shirtsleeves were moving through the Baltimore-Washington International Airport. The crowds just seemed to part for us; I'm sure we were quite a sight. The airlines took very good care of us, advancing us through security, which was nice because we were new amputees and the waiting part could be painful.

When we got to the Denver airport, it was like the president had arrived on concourse B. There was red, white, and blue confetti and balloons everywhere. Crowds of people were gathered in this roped-off area. Little old ladies who were married to American Legion guys, super patriotic, were everywhere. They had cookies and soda and couldn't do enough for us. We were very appreciative. All I could think was, *Wow, this is awesome but overwhelming at the same time.* I didn't want to tear up.

Eventually, it was time to fly us from Denver to Aspen, and we arrived there to meet another eighty volunteers. We were now in a mountain setting, a place called Wildwood in Snowmass Village. I started seeing ladies with frilly necklines, tights, and mink coats. I'd never seen these kind of outfits. I saw couples with matching clothes, too.

We were kind of an elite group ourselves, but in a different way. You had to be really banged up to be invited to this event. There was strict criteria: you had to be missing a limb, paralyzed, or have a severe burn or a head injury. There were some guys from Vietnam who were missing both legs and an arm, and they were skiing. Guys missing both legs from Korea. Wild old men and they were still skiing.

Me and the others from Walter Reed rolled into that event thinking we were expert amputees, but we found out we didn't know anything. We had never been around any amputees except for ourselves, so they gave us a little bit of an education.

One guy wheeled in and said, "Hey, how you doing?" He grabbed a lady with his hook. He was maybe sixty-five or seventy, sitting upright in his chair, very proud. He said he was in the Marine Corps.

I said, "Marine Corps guy, semper fi." I knew that much.

Right away, he asked, "So what happened?" They were all very blunt, very direct. His wife was looking at me, and she said she'd been with him for thirty-seven years. "We do all kinds of stuff together." I realized that they were trying to plant in our minds that everything was okay and we could live normal lives without quite saying, "Hey, cripple, it's going to be all right. We've been together forever, and he took me here and there."

It was interesting. I was studying these veterans and watching how they moved their wheelchairs. They were very fluid because they had been in them a long time. But they didn't have nice equipment. We had all these high-tech wheelchairs, high-tech legs. Some of us were still kind of muscled up at that point, starting to get our shape back. And we were way younger. Here we were, meeting this older generation, one that wasn't taken care of or appreciated. They didn't get ski trips in their day; they weren't given the best equipment. From then on, I felt for the older vets, the Vietnam vets especially.

We had some very eye-opening conversations, and they gave me new perspective. It's human nature to think that the next generation under you is soft. To refer to "this Nintendo generation" or "that entitlement generation." But we have a lot to learn from each other. World War I was terrible. World War II was really, really bad. Korea was awful. Vietnam was really bad. But I bet you that ten years from now, those people are probably going to admit that Iraq and Afghanistan were pretty bad, too, even if they weren't as bad as the other generations' wars. I've heard a lot of Vietnam war stories. I've heard a lot about the bushes exploding with gunfire and people being hit. They were much more vicious and effective fighters than we had faced, and they practiced the same guerrilla warfare that the Americans invented.

The difference is, when you kill somebody in Iraq, you're going to shoot them, you're going to watch them fall, and you're going to remember. When you go walking the streets and somebody chucks a grenade or somebody yells "Allahu Akbar" (God is great) and starts running around the corner spraying, that's very intimate. We didn't lose the same number of troops they did. In another war, I know I would have been one of those numbers—and I knew these men I was meeting were extremely lucky to be here today. We've got better equipment now, better training. We're more effective at communicating, shooting, moving, getting a guy out who is going to live and live a great life, versus die in a rice paddy. And our country was very good to us when we came home.

In a lot of ways, we felt bad for some of the people we met from other wars. We felt like the silver-spoon generation they accused us of being. But we were still blown up. It still sucks.

I loved the guys I met, but I felt their resentment. Some of them said it direct: "Nothing against you guys, but man, we didn't have all this stuff you have." I got it. At least a dozen guys pulled me aside and let me know how great we've got it. We know. We're not dumb. Come on. But we really respect them, and they have lived so many lives compared to us, they have been fathers and business owners. They have already made all the mistakes that we will someday make. I wanted to know about their setbacks so I could hopefully avoid making some of those mistakes, because I hate making mistakes. I make them all the time, obviously, but still, anything you could tell me to make my life better, go ahead and start talking. I want to hear it.

There were also guys at the sports clinic who were hurt the year before and had come on their own. There were maybe forty-five people who had been to Iraq that I could talk to. There were guys from all different walks of military life. You had everyone from Special Forces to regular Army, Navy, Marine, and Air Force. Anybody who had been hurt. We were meeting out there to go skiing, and these little old ladies were smothering us with attention.

CHAPTER 22
Slopes and Amputees

When we checked in, they gave us each a packet with instructions on where we were supposed to be and when. A therapist from Walter Reed was our group leader. He was strict on the instructions and spoke seriously, "You have to be back here at *this* time." I thought, *All right, all right. Calm down.* We all went to our rooms and showered. I had to take my leg off and clean my stump, relube, and eat a few pain pills, then put the prosthetic back on. I was a six-hundred-milligrams-of-Motrin guy; I didn't take Oxycontin or gorilla biscuit, which is what we called Percocet. I knew some who were having a hard time getting off opioids. Many of the guys were on heavy doses of methadone. And we were all on blood thinners to reduce blood clots in our lungs. We were really messed up, but we were not missing this trip.

We went down to the first meeting, which was in a big conference area with hundreds and hundreds of people. They said the next morning we would meet in the same room and be processed. It felt like I was going into the Army again. I was in the third group, which I didn't like because I'm not much for sleeping in. They had a wonderful breakfast set up for us the next morning, a huge buffet, so I grabbed a plate and found a table.

Another old veteran greeted me. "Hi, who are you?"

I introduced myself. "Staff Sergeant Murphy, 101st, two tours, Iraq."

He said, "IED?"

"Oh, yeah. Those things are nasty."

He agreed, "Yeah, they are." He said it was his eighteenth year with the sports clinic and then pointed to the wall. "I'm a sponsor." That's when I realized they had all these levels—gold, silver, bronze. I saw some of the biggest companies in the country represented, all making it possible for me to be there. I met VA people from several states, and there were semitrucks full of equipment. Each skier had three or four people assigned to them, volunteers from all over the world—New Zealand, Canada, and from the States—Vermont, Maine, New York. All were here to help 392 of us, severely wounded service members from all wars.

After breakfast, I was given a bracelet and T-shirt with my group colors. It was very organized, very structured. I started going through the check-in stations. They would look me up. "Murphy, 1234, O-negative." They had all my medical records, in case something happened to me. At each station, you'd hear about the activities: rock climbing, trapshooting, wheelchair fencing. One thing was sled hockey, and I knew I could sit on a sled, maybe rough up some of the others a little. They even had scuba diving in the pool. I thought, *Scuba diving in Aspen? No!* I'm from Florida, I've snorkeled my whole life. So I registered for something else.

They cut us free after we were signed up, and all I had to do was show up the next day at my exact time where I was supposed to meet my instructors. I had a little time to kill, so I went out to see the ones already on the slopes. They were putting together sleds and rigs that I'd never seen before. They had a stand-up rig for a skier who was blind. It was kind of like a shopping cart, and the skier held on to this T-bar. I had seen videos of them wrecking, and it looked pretty bad when they got tangled up in the metal. But eventually the blind skiers can ski without anything in front, just a guy behind him shouting directions, "Left! Right!" They might get them close to the edge of huge drop-offs. "Right! Right! Bail! Bail! Bail!" Bail means go down. Eventually, you'd see a blind skier just skiing effortlessly, making gorgeous turns with a look of thrill on his face the whole way down. I thought, *If he can do that, I can make my little lawn chair ski go, too.*

I was assigned to the second shift for skiing and had all the appropriate gear on, long johns and layers. I was wearing a pair of hiking boots that a peer-mentoring couple from Walter Reed bought me for the trip. The sports clinic had given me a helmet and some outriggers, which are like forearm crutches with a ski at the bottom.

They started us on this big wooden deck they'd built, sheets of plywood on top of pallets with carpet on top. That way they could just push us off the carpet onto the slopes. I looked up and saw the chairlift overhead. A guy smacked his skis to make ice fall on me and we both laughed. There was music, people were wearing Mardi Gras beads, it was kind of a party atmosphere. I'm sure in Snowmass Village it would be weird to see a disabled skier normally, but here there were hundreds of us in this big launching area. I looked at all the rigs and hoped I would get a fast one. It was like when you're a kid and looking at all the go-carts. *Don't give me the crummy one, all right, dude?*

Everyone had these light attitudes. They wanted to know who you were and what the hell happened to you. They were making us all talk about it. I realize now this was different from those other wars. We learned something. They wanted us all to talk about it and get it out.

* * *

The first day skiing, you're learning how to move your hips and how to turn. I had skied some as a kid and was a natural at it, but this was way different. They kept the skier on a big, long tether so they could control our speed. This was Aspen; you could get going really fast in a dangerous direction, and if somebody wasn't on that tether, you could just go off a ledge and be killed. It was well patrolled.

Finally, it was my turn. I was assigned to a guy named Robert Reynolds, and he pointed to one of the rigs, a bi-ski. It had a chair with two skis under it so it was harder to flip over. He said, "This is your sled here."

Next to it was an adaptive mono-ski. That had a chair with metal attached to a normal ski. I said, "Thanks, but I was told that I could use the mono-ski."

Reynolds said, "Yeah, yeah, by the end of the week, we'll try, we'll talk about it. But today you're going to go on the bi-ski."

I knew that putting me on a bi would be less work for all of us, but I said, "Sir, I've only got three days to ski, and those are half days. I'd like to get on that mono, and I was told that if I wanted to do the mono, they'd let me."

His voice turned more military-like. "Listen, I'm in charge. I'm the instructor. You're going on the bi-ski."

About that time, I saw the guy from the hospital, Sandy Trombetta, walk up. He said, "What's the problem?"

Reynolds explained it. "I informed Staff Sergeant Murphy that he's going to be going on a bi-ski, and he wants a mono-ski."

Trombetta said, "That's fine. Put him on a mono."

I didn't say anything. I knew I'd won, but I was going to be with this guy Reynolds all day, so I needed him to get over it. Still, I was thinking, *You lose. I'm getting a mono-ski, and you'd better be able to keep up!*

The team helped me get situated on the seat of the mono-ski, and it was uncomfortable as hell—and wobbly. I didn't fit, so they were trying to get some pads here and adjustments there, tightening this strap, loosening that one. I had to hold myself up with the outriggers while they were adjusting me. I did what they said, "Get up, scoot up." My left foot was strapped to a foothold in front of the chair, so I was balancing my body on the thin ski below.

They told me I needed to have my head, hips, and toes downrange. "Think of it like you're driving from your belly button." I thought, *I can do that. Good coaching there. Got it. Boom. Downrange. Go.* He continued, "Then, when you want to make a turn, just reach out with the outrigger. If you want to go right, use the right hand, and it's kind of like you're opening a door. So open the door." He demonstrated the movement for me. "The belly button follows the door, so you turn to the right." I thought, *Follow the belly button, head downrange. I got this.*

Reynolds latched two yellow nylon tethers onto each side of my seat and said he would stay about ten feet behind me to monitor my speed and direct me away from big drop-offs. He said, "You ready?"

I shifted in the seat a little and said, "Yeah!"

He said, "All right. Go!"

I started to launch and immediately fell over. *Crap.* I thought I could at least get farther out. I knew some of my buddies were watching and clearly enjoying the entertainment. So now I was out of position, and they had to undo the straps and get me resituated, get the pads in place, and secure the straps again. My upper-body strength wasn't great at this point, and the altitude was getting to me a little. I felt some pain, too, but figured, *We'll get this right. Keep your head down and go.*

When I was set again, I heard Reynolds: "You ready? Go!" This time, I went twenty feet and boom, it was over. I didn't feel like I'd learned anything. The third time, I was at least able to make it all the way down to the bottom, slowly. I heard Reynolds behind me, "Open the door! Open the door!" Then I saw this little kid zip by me, cutting me off, and here I was on this tether. But I would get there.

I could sense Reynolds behind me trying to feel things out. I'd start going faster, and he would back me down. As I moved, he would move, and it affected the angle of my ski, so we were learning how to work together. And this was the easiest bunny slope you could ever imagine. It was bottom of the hill, right in front of the place we'd go drink beer afterward. Everybody was watching. *This is Murph's first start*, on the easy slope, with a guy tethered behind me and two other instructors on skis, one on my left and another on my right yelling things at me. They were helpful, I just had to learn.

Next, they were going to load me on the chairlift to get to another slope. They said it could be dangerous. I had been watching the lift swing by, scooping up skiers who just fell back into it sitting down. It was different when you were strapped into a chair on top of a single ski. The guys helping people get on and off the lift looked like college grads who didn't want to grow up. They had their loud music playing, with big grins and terrible tan lines on their faces from being out on the slopes all winter. But they were all very positive. They said they would slow down the lift and count down—three-two-one—and I would lift up on the outriggers, and they would pull me back into the chair. *And oh, by the way, if you don't make it, the chair's going to run over you and crush you into the ground, which will make everybody freak out, and you don't want any special attention, right?*

As if everybody wasn't already looking at us guys with all the special equipment and missing limbs. The place was loaded with people from all over the best places in America, and there were Argentinians, and then there was us. We were slowing down the lines and holding things up.

There was a D-ring on the back of the mono-ski seat, and they said once they had me on the lift, they were going to latch it. Reynolds, who was going to be riding with me, said, "We've also got to remember to unlatch it, or you're going to be hanging from the lift." A lot of things could go wrong here. But it was all worth it. Compared to life at Walter Reed? I was willing to take any risk they'd give me.

I got into place, and they started counting then held the chair back and launched me right onto the seat. And away we went. I started trying to shift in the seat, but Reynolds said, "You're on there pretty good." He was D-ringing me to the bar, and I said, "Don't forget that." He's said, "Oh, no. We've been warned a million times. I've got you." Then he added, "But if I do, you're not going anywhere! Ha, ha, ha." He took off his gloves and put them under his right leg and took his poles and put them under his left leg, and leaned back. He was all comfortable like this was his golf. I started wondering if I should be scared.

We talked a little and got to know each other. We talked about attitude, life, comebacks. He told me his story about being in Special Forces and being injured in a parachute accident. He broke his back, but worked really hard and was able to walk again. And the guy could ski. We were bonding, and I was able to loosen up.

We got to the top, and I went down the slope and didn't fall much at all. Reynolds gave me a lot of compliments and was helping me improve. I was carving the snow better and faster. I had changed my approach of driving with my belly button and was instead driving under my butt. If I hit a bump, I needed to land it right there. To initiate turns, I started with the stump or the leg. Not so much opening the door, like he said, because that kept putting me in a bad position. But the head and chest downrange was good. I found the belly button to be a good aiming point, but not a good steering point.

It reminded me of being in a wrestling match and stepping into a man, to blow into him. It took the same balance and torqueing move. Yeah, I was getting better and better, and it felt great. Reynolds and I did some more runs together and were becoming good buddies. I told him I wanted to go to the top my first day. He was adamant—I was doing really well, but there were plenty of great greens and even some easy blues that I was already seeing that first day. When we got to the end, I begged them to let me go back up again, but they wouldn't. We called it a day.

When I woke up the next morning, I was in the worst pain. The muscles that I had used on the mono-ski were pretty broken down. I wondered if I had overdone it and was a little nervous. So I kept eating my six hundred milligrams of ibuprofen, and I was pounding the water. I soaked in the bathtub, but I was still in a lot of pain.

The next time I got to the slopes, Reynolds seemed happy to see me again. When the team sat me down on the chair, I was in tons of pain—my butt was bruised. I had become kind of bony on the backside during my hospital stay, and what muscles I had left weren't worth much. I felt terrible. But I sucked it up and we went skiing.

We went to the top! Not the black diamonds, but we went all the way to the top on all the lifts, the hard blues included. Reynolds was ecstatic. When my session was over that day, I hung around hoping someone else would cancel. And one guy did. I told the instructors, "Oh, please! Please?" They took me, and I got to meet more of the volunteers. I was really impressed with them, and they seemed surprised this was my first time ever mono-skiing. I made their jobs easier. I wanted to do more and more. I hit jumps, hit powder, and I went between the trees. I told them I wanted to ski a black diamond, but they said, "No, absolutcly not. No." That would have to be another trip.

Since then, I've almost killed myself on a mono-ski. I've been so many times now, most recently in Montana. Through my short ski career, people have called me a two-turn skier. I turn at the top to go down and then turn at the bottom when I'm done. That's not really true, I can make nice turns, but sometimes I like to let it go a little bit and feel that edge, that side that scares you. I always peel it back before I get scared, but my version of getting scared is way past every-one else's, so most people think I'm crazy.

I didn't know it, but at the end of the Winter Sports Clinic, they hold a recognition dinner, and I received the inspirational award. It included notes that the instructors had written about me—it was very, very touching. It came with an all-expense paid trip back to Aspen, with a guest. I was pretty self-conscious receiving the award, consid-ering there were guys with worse injuries than mine, including dou-ble amputees. For the first time out of the hospital, *everybody* was doing great. It wasn't just me.

CHAPTER 23
Ice Hockey and Paybacks

There was a lieutenant colonel from Walter Reed with us on that Winter Sports Clinic trip. He was a pilot who eventually became one of the first to fly an aircraft in active-duty Air Force with one leg amputated above the knee. Lieutenant Colonel Andrew Lourake was a group leader, kind of a peer mentor for us. He knew every single wounded guy, and everybody knew him and his wife, Lisa. She used to flirt with us. Of course, she was just messing around, but she was very pretty. Andrew and Lisa would go to every steak dinner, every event. They were very involved and kept us all positive. Andrew was always tough and stern, but gentle when he needed to be, and he was a good listener. If he was in charge, you didn't mess around.

There was another tough guy named Neil Duncan who was a double amputee. He was in my group, which was being bussed over to play sled hockey. Neil always had an attitude with me, and I had one right back. We both looked around the bus, and it was clear we were going to have to be on the same team. Either that or we were going to kill each other, so we made an alliance. We would be on the same team.

When we got off the bus, we were introduced to a guy who was a member of the United States Paralympic Sled Hockey Team. He talked about how he'd lost both his legs as a child and how he had grown up without having anything. When he discovered ice hockey, he finally had something he was really good at, something he could compete in. It gave him pride and purpose in his life.

The organizers broke us up in teams and sent us into the locker room to put on our pads. Everybody had a helmet and a tiny stick. I looked at that thing and thought, *I want a big stick!* It seemed pointless to be so close to the ground, strapped to a narrow sled, with this small stick. Someone said that the bottom of the stick had spikes that you used to propel yourself across the ice, then make a shot. When we first got out there, we weren't going very fast and could hardly turn. It was really awkward. That Paralympic guy was flying around, zipping in and out of us. He wasn't going to be competing, though, that wouldn't be fair.

I looked over and saw that the lieutenant colonel, Andrew, was on the other team. I glanced at Neil, and he had noticed it, too. I sledded toward Andrew as fast as I could go, which wasn't fast at all, and trucked him with my forearm—*bam!* Nailed him. He went down hard. Then here comes Neil. He flies up and nails him, too. The officials were blowing the whistle, and I heard, "Stop! Stop!" I grabbed the front of Andrew's sled and lifted it up, so he was flat on his back, he couldn't get upright. Like a turtle. I was holding him there, and his wife Lisa was yelling at me from the stands. One of the other guys came and pulled me off and helped Andrew get back upright. He turned to me and said, "Knock it off. Play the game."

So we started playing again, and I saw another chance—*boom!* Clotheslined him. I grabbed the front of his sled and jerked it up real hard. Sure enough, he was back in his turtle position. He couldn't get up and he was cussing. Neil was loving it. He came by and nailed both of us, so Andrew fell on his side and was able to get up. Lisa was yelling at us from the bleachers, "Neil! Luke! Cut it out!"

Neil and I got up speed and nailed him again. He started trying to fight back, and other guys on his team were trying to attack us, but

Neil and I were too tough, we were flipping all of them on their backs like turtles.

One of the officials said, "Guys, it's hockey, not turtles. Just play the game." I saw that the lieutenant colonel had had enough, and we were getting yelled at, so we backed off. Then I looked over to the corner of the ice and saw Jim Nicholson, the secretary of Veterans Affairs. I looked at Neil, and it was like, *Oh, it's on.* We started racing toward him. I got there first and clotheslined him. That's when I saw the Secret Service scaling the walls and running toward me. Guess what? That game was over. No more turtling. Kind of ruined it for me.

We started playing regular hockey, and it was horrible. Terrible. It's hard to go fast, and you think you have this perfect shot, but you slip and fall. It's just really awkward. It must have taken that Paralympian years to get as good as he was—I give him all the credit in the world for the way he moved on the ice. Me? I was just out there to fight because that's all I'd ever seen on TV and it was fun. I thought it was legal. Apparently, it was not legal or fun (for everyone else).

The next night, I received an invitation to a fancy dinner in Aspen. I thought, *Why would they invite me to dinner?* But I went. I wasn't going to say no. I was there kind of on orders anyway, so I showed up for the dinner. I was wearing my nicest clothes, but I hadn't really packed anything for something this formal. I was way out of place. When I walked in, the host said, "Your table is over there, Mr. Murphy." I walked over and realized I was at Jim Nicholson's table. All those friggin' Secret Service jokers were going to attack me again. I looked around and saw that my chair was right next to his. I thought, *Oh, how convenient.* To my right was another VIP, the president of the World Bank, Paul Wolfowitz. Then it was all these highfalutin folks.

They served dinner, and I was having a glass of red wine and trying to be polite, but I was in no way, shape, or form ready for this kind of setting. I had tact, and I wasn't going to mess this up, though, so I was taking small bites and using my best manners. *I've got this. No problem.*

Nicholson started talking about how the VA was trying really hard to get these prosthetic legs better. I thought, *These legs are the best they've been, dude. They're good.* He said he was really interested in the foot technology and understood that the above-the-knee amputees didn't have quite the feet that the below-the-knees amputees did, because there was too much movement and it bucked the knee. I thought, *Yeah, you're right, it's unfortunate. Yeah, I already know that; you're singing to the choir.* Then he turned to me and said, "Do you mind showing me what you've got, Luke? Your fake foot?"

I said, "Um, right now?" I was thinking, *I'm at dinner, and I'm trying real hard not to be a redneck here, and you want the shoe off?* It was close to an order, so I said, "Well, yes, sir." Everybody at the table was looking, and so I pushed my chair back, took my shoe off, and showed it to them. But as I was looking, I saw something red on the toes. I thought, *Ah! I'm bleeding!* But it was a fake foot, I couldn't be bleeding. It was a strange reaction, I know. I looked closer and realized somebody had painted the toenails on my fake foot.

I was mortified. I glanced up and saw Andrew with this huge grin on his face, and I thought, *Oh, you bastard.* He totally got me back. The secretary started laughing and everyone else did, too. They were all in on it. It was pretty funny. They got me good.

I figured out later how it happened. Since I took my leg off every time I went skiing, after the sled hockey incident, Andrew captured it, took the shoe off, and painted all the toenails hot pink. It made me realize that when you mess with people, watch out—they can get you back. And they might be better at it than you are.

But all is forgiven now. When Homes for Our Troops built a home for me in 2013, Andrew and Lisa surprised me by attending the dedication. I had not seen them since Walter Reed. It made me almost cry. He also told this same story in front of a crowd of people at that event, including a US congressman. It's now official history.

CHAPTER 24
Meeting Mary

This lady named Mary Bryant McCourt came to Walter Reed one day and said she wanted us to train for a marathon. She was so bubbly and nice, we kind of discounted the fact that we all thought she was crazy.

Mary is nearly six feet tall, somewhere in her forties, and has been an international model. She has this huge still-on-a-stage kind of smile. She talks to you with her smile. "Oh, hey, happy. How are you doing?" She was like a recruiter walking around Walter Reed. She told us to go to the ground-floor foyer at a particular time, and she would have these handicapped bikes for us to try out.

The physical therapists were talking up the bikes, too, but I was a little skeptical. Until I saw this girl amputee with an awesome black eye. Crystal also had a cut on her face and maybe a broken nose. She looked like she'd gotten sucker-punched. I said, "What happened to your face?"

Crystal, also an IED victim, was missing a leg, and her other leg was jacked up like mine. She was in a wheelchair. "I was riding one of Mary's bikes. I didn't realize you couldn't turn real fast, and I went into a concrete bench face first."

I said, "Did you have a helmet on?"

She said, "Yeah, but it didn't protect my face." She smiled with her messed-up face, and I thought, *Oh, man.*

I went downstairs where Mary was doing her demonstration and went right up to her. "What are you doing? You come here to the hospital and you hurt Crystal?"

Mary put her hand over her mouth, embarrassed, and said, "We're so sorry she hit that bench." She dropped her head a little, and I knew I had her.

I said, "I saw her face."

She looked at me and winced. "It's bad, isn't it?"

I was trying to give my serious look, which was hard because Mary's eyes are so cheerful. "It's really bad. Are you going to let me get hurt like that?"

Mary shook her head. "No, no." She saw my smile, and we both laughed. Who could be mad at Mary?

The whole time I was messing with her, all these guys were just zipping around, going real fast with these hand-crank bikes.

I got on one and gave it a try. I thought, *I could probably get pretty good at this.* On the hand-crank bikes, you push forward and pull back with both arms in a circular motion at the same time—forward, forward, forward. The stronger you pull, the faster it goes. It's hard, especially on your shoulders. It's tough to get going, and then once you get going, you can't turn too fast or you'll flip, like Crystal did.

Mary told us about the Achilles Freedom Team of Wounded Veterans that she'd started. The group's main purpose was to raise awareness that people with disabilities can still do things. She matched people like us with adaptable equipment to overcome our injuries and hopefully go on to compete. The hand-crank bikes could be expensive, like five thousand dollars each, so Achilles helps by making them available to you. She said if we wanted to compete in a marathon, Achilles would fly us to the event, pay our hotel and food, and we would race as a team. The goal wasn't to win, although some of the team members finished in the top of their age group.

Mary left about ten bikes behind in the gym for us. She said, "Please use them."

One day I ran into my Snowmass turtling buddy, Neil Duncan, who lost both of his legs in Afghanistan. He was in the 173rd Airborne, which is a very tough unit, like the 101st. They probably thought they were better than us, and of course we know that we're better than anybody. That's just the mentality of the infantry. Neil had a tracheotomy scar on his neck and scars on his lip going down into his chin. All his teeth were blown out, and his jaw was broken. He had metal where his teeth used to be, eventually crowned. His legs had been so mangled, the doctors had amputated both, one above the knee and one below. Neil liked to call me a wimp for not getting my other leg chopped off, because he was up walking in no time, and I was in a chair forever, miserable with a rotten leg.

Neil said he was going riding that afternoon. Mary had left bikes behind for us in the gym. He said we could sign the bikes out from the gym. I said, "I'll go. I'll meet you there."

At about three that afternoon, I was already worn out. I wasn't getting out a lot at that point, but here I was about to ride bikes with the craziest son of a bitch at Walter Reed. Neil always walked faster and harder than anybody else. He was from Minnesota and was a hockey player. After steak dinners on Friday nights, we'd all get in the bus and go home to get some sleep. Neil would take a cab out and hit bars, walk around the icy streets with both legs gone. This guy had been through the ringer, but it wasn't slowing him down.

If anybody complained around Neil, he'd just look at you like, *Stop whining*. He used to give me attitude even though he was a sergeant and I was a staff sergeant, so I outranked him. Of course, that doesn't matter, nobody cares about rank at Walter Reed. It's how long you've been there and how bad you're hurt. At the end of the day, he knew and I knew— that's all that mattered. He was bigger than me. His body was harder and tougher than mine. I'm glad we never had to find out how tough.

We checked out the bikes and went zipping out of the parking lot. I definitely wanted to keep up. Neil had on a backpack and earphones, and looked like he'd been doing this a few times a week, but this was my first time leaving the hospital campus on a bike. I figured if he went fast, I would just remember the route so I could make it back on my own. That didn't happen. Neil started going fast, so I went fast. He went faster; I went faster. I wasn't paying attention to where we were going. I was going through all these hills, and I followed when he turned into Rock Creek Park. It was beautiful but very hilly, with creeks in the middle, like Central Park in New York City. I saw a huge buck with a giant rack in the same park when I visited months later. It's a good thing I don't live in Washington, because I would be in that park with my bow and arrow.

Neil kept flying, and I was trying to keep up. I was going down a hill and trying to get some steam, maybe gain on him. I got to the bottom of the hill, and there was a sharp turn and I didn't know it. I hit the brakes, but I couldn't slow down fast enough. I was probably going forty-five miles an hour. I tried to slow to about twenty-five. I leaned and turned left and went up on one wheel and started rolling, still strapped to the bike. My head hit the pavement, and I was glad I was wearing a helmet. I started rolling—*boom, boom*—and then I went off the side of the hill and rolling through the leaves. I felt a rip in my hamstring on my stump. I kept rolling: bike, face, bike, face, roll, roll, roll. I must have rolled thirty times before I finally hit the bottom—the bike went one way and I went the other. As soon as I stopped, I grabbed my leg and then realized it was just a cramp. I thought, *Okay, I'm all right.* I stretched it out and it was better. *I'm good.* I knew my face was scratched up and dirty, I had blood in my teeth—and leaves. I had literally eaten the dirt on the way down. It was a pretty violent crash.

I realized I was going to have to push the bike up the steep slope. That meant crawling with my fake leg because I still had the cage on my good leg at the time. I yelled, "Neil!" No Neil. No people. I was in the middle of nowhere in the park, and my bike was all jacked up. I found a rock, so I would push the bike, put the rock down to hold it in place, crawl a little, push the bike, crawl—it was working. I finally made it 150 feet to the very top.

About that time, Neil came cranking up. I could tell he was pissed off because he had to backtrack and find me. When he saw me dragging myself across the ground, he didn't say anything. He looked down at the disturbed leaves, the trail I'd made toward the creek, and said, "You all right?"

I nodded. "Yeah."

He said, "You want to go back?"

I said, "Yeah." I got back on the bike and started cranking, but it wasn't going very fast. I think I bent the tire.

We came to an intersection and had to wait for the crosswalk. These dudes were sitting on a bench waiting on the bus, and one of them turned to me. "Damn, man. You all right?" I didn't know what I looked like, but I could feel the dirt in my teeth. My lip was busted. I knew I had scratches on my face, like a cat had nailed me a few times. I said, "Yeah, I'm fine."

When we got to Walter Reed, a security guard stopped us. "I need to see your ID."

"My what?" I said. "I'm a patient here!"

"Then show me your ID."

I said, "No, get out of my way," and started wheeling past the gate.

I could hear sarcastic Neil behind me. "Yeah, you have to have your ID, man."

I went upstairs and parked the bike and ran into one of my buddies. "What the hell happened to you?"

I said, "I went for a bike ride with Neil Duncan." He understood.

Since my face was all messed up, word started getting around, so Mary called me. I said, "See? You got Crystal all screwed up and then you got me all screwed up. They're talking about taking the bikes away."

She said, "Oh, no, really?" I hesitated a moment to keep her in suspense. Then told her I was only kidding and added, "But they are dangerous as hell."

She laughed. The marathon recruitment process had begun.

CHAPTER 25

Man of Steele

The 101st Airborne has a liaison at Walter Reed who looks out for our guys. He came by one day and said, "Hey, Sergeant Murphy, aren't you a Rakkasan?" He contacted my unit and let them know how I was doing. Months later, the Rakkasan brigade commander, Colonel Mike Steele, came to my room during his midtour leave.

Normally, you never see the brigade commander, and you don't *want* to see the battalion commander. Those guys never shoot their weapon; they're looking at the screen and moving men. You don't talk to them, and when they're around, you're in a position of attention. They are untouchable and have nothing to do with guys like me on the enlisted side.

Steele was different, he was more hands-on. He took over as commander of the 101st Airborne Division's Third Brigade (Rakkasans) in June 2004 and oversaw the transformation of the unit from the traditional three-battalion infantry brigade into a six-battalion infantry brigade combat team, including reconnaissance. He was decorated from Somalia, when he was Captain Steele, and served in Afghanistan as a lieutenant colonel with the Tenth Mountain Division. When he took over the Rakkasans, he was a full-blown colonel, and he went with us to Iraq.

I didn't expect the colonel to visit me at Walter Reed, but I wasn't surprised when he did. What little I knew about him, he seemed like the type who would definitely go see his men. Still, he's the only colonel I know who visited his wounded.

Steele had thousands under him, so it's not like he knew me, but he said he did remember me from the field. He was around a lot when we trained. One of the first times I saw him in the field was when he took over. We were at Fort Campbell, and we were doing a mini survival, evasion, resistance, escape (SERE) school, which is used to give the younger guys an idea of what it might actually be like if they got captured by the enemy. We had built a mock POW camp, and some of our own guys dressed up as Iraqis. The "prisoners" were on their knees with sandbags over their heads by a campfire. The test was to respond according to the rules of engagement. They could give only their name, rank, and serial number. If they gave anything else, they were disobeying a direct order. We saw Steele watching from the top of the hill in his Humvee. He told our leaders, "This has got to be the stupidest shit I've ever seen. Get these guys doing something better than this!" He meant get us back to normal line infantry, like squad attack, shooting and clearing buildings.

Steele was something to watch around the base. He'd grab the biggest dumbbells in the gym and bench them. He also had a tarantula in a cage in his office. He was a turkey hunter, duck hunter, deer hunter. He drove this old green Ford with a rope wrapped around the bumper in an X and had duck calls hanging from the rearview mirror. Most officers had very practical vehicles, or if they were a little fancy, they might have a Beemer. They make a lot more money than we do.

One of the nicknames we had for Steele was "Big Hungry." He looked like Shrek. He had legs like tree trunks—he was huge. Still, even as a forty-year-old man, at 270 pounds, he could run fifteen miles no problem.

When Steele first came to the Rakkasans, I didn't know much about him. I only knew that one by one, guys who had been there for a while started leaving, saying things like, "Oh, man, Steele's a ball-breaker, dude. We're out of here." Some had been Rangers, so we're all thinking, *How bad is this guy?*

I knew that he'd been a University of Georgia offensive lineman turned Army Ranger. You've got to be able to do a certain number of pull-ups to even get into Ranger school, and then to be a Ranger you've got to be able to scale a rope. How many offensive linemen right now in college football do you think can do enough pull-ups to be a Ranger? If there's another one, I'd be shocked.

It's also rare to have a big guy in the infantry. We're all usually strong but don't need to be real big. It's not fun to carry a big guy when he's wounded. He's also a bigger target. You don't have to be real broad to carry a backpack and shoot people. You can be a little guy, or tall, but not too tall.

Immediately, there were going to be some changes under Steele. No more running for only one hour and then playing basketball to get a little cardio and build camaraderie. No more basketball, period. *Whoa. No more basketball?!*

In recon, all of us could run seven miles in thirty-five minutes. Seven miles a day was good enough exercise. We would do some stretching, some push-ups and sit ups, do some sprints up a hill, carry a guy up a hill, then play basketball for fifteen minutes to cool down. But not anymore, not under the colonel. So now we had to run for an hour and a half. We had to slow ourselves down because blowing in eleven, twelve miles on a regular basis led to injuries. Everyone was pretty mad at Steele for a while.

He made the change permanent. He took the basketball courts and had them covered in rubber pads. *Oh, well, guess he was serious.* Then he had the baskets removed and replaced them with a wooden sign that said, Small Arm Repair Shop—his idea of a gym. He had a bunch of weights brought in, and now the basketball court was a weight room, which was nice because the previous one wasn't big enough. He hung these motivational signs and worked out in there. You'd see him grab the 140-pound dumbbells that most of us couldn't even pick up, walk over with those big damn legs to a bench, lie down, and just start pressing them. No problem. Anyone want to mess with the colonel? No? All right then. Just run your hour and a half and forget the basketball. *Got it.*

* * *

I'd always had a problem with the chow hall guys. I was only 180 pounds at this time, and I was lifting weights every day, eating right, and trying to get in the best shape possible, but the chow hall guys were stingy. We'd get up at four or five in the morning and wouldn't eat because we were going to do a fourteen-mile run for Steele. After showering, it would be seven forty-five or eight in the morning, and we'd be starving when we got to chow hall. I'm sure it's not easy making food for thousands of men—the cooks had a tough job. But it was clear their priorities were not the same as ours. They'd give me a half scoop of this and a half scoop of that—really skimp on the food. And I'd outrank the guy serving by a couple of ranks, but he's a cook and I'm just a grunt in the line.

That all ended when Colonel Steele got there. It was the first cool thing that happened. He'd stand by the line and say, "Give him more. Did you hear me, son?" He'd order the cook to get his leadership, and then a lieutenant would be out there serving the chow line. *Guess what, buddies? That's an infantry colonel. He knows we're working our tails off and knows we've got to eat.* Then next thing you know, we're having a steak night. Then a steak and lobster night. It was frozen, but what a change.

I liked Steele's approach. He probably realized an Army marches on its belly. When you're training these guys, you're beating them down. They need to be fed. If a guy's fat, well, cut him back. But some of these guys are like twigs. They're like me when I was seventeen or eighteen. Steele understood we didn't need a guy on the chow line holding back.

One day Steele said, "Rakkasans, Week of the Eagles is coming." You could hear our collective grunt. That's when all the brigades of the 101st Airborne come together for a series of competitions. There would be boxing, combatives, a ten-mile run, a twenty-five-mile ruck march/race. There were competitions between all the machine gunners, the snipers, and the pistol shooters. He continued in his characteristic growl, "We will not be competing in badminton or basketball." We all snickered. "But we will win every fighting event, every run, every shooting event." And we did. We won them all. Swept them up. That's because he fed us. That's because he instilled in us that we knew we worked harder than anyone else in that whole division. Everybody else got to play basketball. We were in the gym more, we were shooting more. We put special emphasis only on those events that were pertinent to our job. We wanted to win in events that really mattered, and we did.

Steele earned our loyalty. We were already proud. Everybody hates the Rakkasans, but we were the first into Afghanistan. We went the furthest into Iraq in '03 in the invasion, and everybody knows it. But when Steele came, he took it to another level. We wanted to win, for us and for him.

* * *

We went on a run once, the whole division. That's about thirty-five thousand men. It was going to be a nightmare. We were told to wear our blue brigade shirts. There were thousands of us, very tightly formed, waiting for the division commander to come by and follow whatever unit was going to be following him. We were standing there for an hour. I was looking to my left, looking for the general—where's the general? Finally, they started coming—a big stream of another color, very tight, running in perfect rows, side-by-side and keeping space in front of them.

I saw Steele coming; he stood out. He just looked different. He looked like he struggled to run, because he didn't look like he should be able to, like a grizzly bear running on two legs. It didn't look natural. But he had this big grin on his face as he came through the blue shirts, because we'd fall in behind him, way behind him—behind the thousands behind him. But when he came through grinning with those big Georgia red cheeks, everybody started getting pumped, all four thousand of us full of adrenaline, like, *He's one of us; we're one and the same.* You're a Rakkasan before you're a Screaming Eagle, and all that inner competition is what makes us great. It may not look right to outsiders, but it makes you the most lethal thing going.

Steele was pure infantryman, but he also knew how to plan and execute well, and he could build an esprit de corps like no colonel I've ever had. He should be a four-star general, but they would never let him. He's too much like Patton. He should be kept in a big glass jar that says, "Break in time of war." He's the guy you want when there's big trouble. Steele is a man's man, a soldier's soldier, an infantryman's colonel.

When we were in Iraq, I heard that Steele made the leaders go examine the bodies with him at the morgue. I never heard of anybody doing that. There was a purpose; he was there to learn and to teach. He'd say, "Look at where he's shot. Look at this hole. It must have hit from the right." If a guy was in a fight, he'd ask, "Why wasn't he squared off with the enemy with his elbows tucked?" They'd have to think it through. "Oh, sir, the guy didn't see it coming. It was an ambush or a sniper." He always wanted to learn something, and he wanted us to learn from it by reliving it, retelling it. Maybe he did it to help soldiers mentally or maybe to bring closure. Or if somebody wasn't taking things seriously enough.

The first time Steele came to see me at Walter Reed, he said, "I want you to know that when you got hit, I flew down personally. I brought my staff, and I inspected your vehicle with First Sergeant Coroy." It wasn't something I was expecting. It's usually guys at my level who go to look at the vehicles, so when I heard he'd done that, it made an impression. "Pretty nasty EFP," he said. "You doing all right?"

We talked, and I gave him a piece of shrapnel out of my leg that I had in a jar. I had about thirty pieces that I gave to people throughout my recovery, sometimes if I got too drunk. I gave the colonel a piece of copper. He knew what it meant, that it was part of the bomb used to blow us up. He held it up to the light and looked a little closer. He said, "Thank you. Thank you, Sergeant Murphy. I'll put this on my mantel." He slid it in his pocket and walked out.

After I'd been at Walter Reed a few months and could move around better, Steele called. "You're the highest-ranking Rakkasan there. I want you to get everybody together, and I want to come see them. I'm going to buy pizza and beer." So he rented a room at the Mologne House, a hotel some of us moved into when we were ready for outpatient treatment. I went around and found all the Rakkasans and told them about it. We got together for pizza and beer about a week later, and he sat with us. He wasn't the big, mean guy we used to work for, he was just like a dad almost, totally different. Of course, if somebody started acting up, he'd stiffen up and give you that big-guy look.

As tough as Steele was on the outside, I saw him around his wife and kid, and he was really gentle. He was hard when he had to be—in combat—then kind of cool when he needed to be. In my mind, that's a normal guy, but it's a hard combination to get in a leader. You get put in a leadership position, and next thing you know, you turn into a prison guard. A little power can go to your head. But Steele was a good balance of everything, a good holy guy. He is a pretty complete dude.

I also respected Colonel Steele because, indirectly, I feared my leaders. They could kill me, they could get me killed. They could send me on a mission that I didn't agree with, but I'd have to do it anyway. If I was told I had to do something, it wasn't, "Uh, I don't think that's a good idea." That's not the Rakkasan way. It helps if you have respect for the person giving the order and trust they are going to at least have your best interests in mind. If you've got a guy in there you don't like, don't respect, that's weighing on you all the time.

We saw the method to Steele's madness. We might have hated his guts at first, but he was good to us, and by the time we went to war, we were ready, and we would have died for the colonel.

CHAPTER 26
Let Me Speak

In April 2007, when I moved back to Stuart, Florida, after leaving Walter Reed, Mary and I kept in touch. She called and said, "Are you riding your bike? Are you training? Because I've got this marathon coming up." She recruited me for the Achilles Team and encouraged me to race my first marathon in nearby Palm Beach.

My dad had sold the home we grew up in, so I was living in a place on the river. I rode through the neighborhood and then on a three-mile stretch. I kept building mileage, and before long I was riding across town. Unfortunately, with the hand-crank bikes, you're low to the ground, about bumper high, so people in cars don't always see you. I came close to getting hit every time I went out. I knew if I *did* get hit, I was going under the vehicle, and would probably be dragged until I was dead.

Marathon training forced me to push through the pain, just like the old days when I was running. My arms got tired really fast because they don't carry oxygen the way legs do. A person can run for hundreds of miles, but pumping with your arms is like walking on your hands for the same mileage. It's murder. The shoulders get weak and you feel your muscles—triceps, biceps, and deltoids—burning. The lats also hurt from all that pulling, and your traps get tight. It's the same motion over and over, you can't change your position. It's just push-pull, push-pull, push-pull. You try to get a breathing rhythm, but you can't do it the way you can with running. Maybe if you go slow, you can do it, but not at the speed you need to win a marathon. Of course,

I was going for the win. I just wanted to finish the first one, but after that I was going to give it a shot.

The area where I lived in South Florida didn't have a lot of hills to practice on. When I went up a hill, I crawled like a snail because it's hard for your arms to push your whole body weight using that little circle pattern. The bikes do have gears —I have about thirty gears on my bike. But still, going uphill with all your weight in the back and the wheel up front doesn't work. Going downhill is easy, of course. You don't have to do anything, and you can get going about fifty miles an hour, so if you're competing, you make those count. I always got killed on the uphills, but I usually caught up with people on the down and into the flats. Every time you make a turn, you'd better do it right. You'd better be on the inside, go in low and come out high. Every second matters.

On my first marathon, my arms were burning at mile nine. I thought, *All right, that's just burn.* I knew sooner or later it would go numb, maybe mile eleven or thirteen. I saw some people giving away PowerGel at one of the water stops, so I slammed a couple. That gave me a burst. There were race volunteers riding on regular bikes, saying, "Keep going!" which also pumped us up. Then I saw more people along the route cheering. That probably carried me the rest of the way. My oldest brother, Eddie, was going to be at the finish line with his family, so I didn't want to quit. I finished it. I have no idea where I was in the lineup, somewhere in the back, but that was fine with me.

One of the guys who beat me had long hair and cranked like I'd never seen before. He had a different kind of bike, a kneeler, and he would throw his whole body forward. On my bike, I just sit and do my arms. I try to use my back muscles, but I definitely don't have my whole body into it. This old guy was a below-the-knee amputee, and kneeling gave him more leverage.

I hadn't done enough training for my first marathon, but I was getting better. I felt a great high after that finish. You know when you're extremely red in the face, but you feel good? I knew from being a runner that the best part about it was being done. Hand cranking was the same way. So I had this great feeling immediately afterward, but then I was sore the whole next week. My arms didn't want to work—I couldn't even lift them to shake a spectator's hand—and my palms had painful bruises from the metal grips. I definitely needed to get some better gloves.

* * *

With a home in Palm Beach and another in New York City, Mary runs with the right crowd to get bikes donated, like the ones she brought to Walter Reed. Her late husband was David McCourt, whose first wife and four-year-old daughter were killed when their plane crashed into the World Trade Center on 9/11. Through David and Mary's contacts, she knew the biggest of the big. Once I started racing with the Achilles Team, Mary asked me to come to a fundraiser she had arranged at the President's Country Club in Palm Beach. It's the type of place where you pay about a half a million to be a member, then you still have to pay for a round of golf. Crazy.

Before the fundraiser started, Mary said, "Luke, this is how we do it. Just work the crowd, talk to everybody. Tell them who you are, and then they'll talk about Achilles during dinner." There were big, big companies there and a lot of the local Palm Beach crowd—over-tanned, dressed fancy, country-club types. Then there were a bunch of blown-up guys who were all scarred to hell, missing arms and legs, rolling around in wheelchairs, smiling and drinking all the free booze.

I was standing in this bar area surrounded by bluebloods. I had never been around folks like this. I was watching them and learning how they move and communicate and act. I obviously had nothing in common with them, but I enjoyed eating really good food, having interesting conversation and drinks in an awesome setting. And I learned a lot.

Donald Trump was talking to the guy next to me, a Marine who lost both his legs up high. Trump was very sincere, very nice, smiling. He's got the hair and everything. I was just checking him out; this was a learning experience for me. I was studying his mannerisms, and then he turned toward me and said, "How are you doing? What's your name? You feel good? You comfortable?" While we were talking, a guy took a photo of us. It was one of those instant cameras, so he handed the photo to me a few minutes later. I looked like I had fish lips because I was talking. I thought, *Man, that can't be my picture with Trump!*

I saw that he was still working the crowd, so I walked up and tapped him on the shoulder, "Mr. Trump?" I waved the photo, kind of quick, and said, "There must have been something with your hair in that pic. Can we get another one?" He gave me that look, like he was onto me. I didn't want to tell him it was me who had the fish lips. He was nice about it and said, "Yeah, yeah, let's get another one. We don't want that." So I ended up getting a really good picture with Donald Trump.

I was sitting at the table with Hall of Fame baseball pitcher Jim Palmer, who may be just as famous for his Jockey underwear commercials. He's six five, and both of us were going to be playing on a foursome the next day. He obviously wanted to talk about golf, and I don't even like golf. My brothers are golf freaks, and I can play. I golf in tournaments if it's a good cause, but it's painful. I usually spend more time chasing the beer girl around, smoking cigars, and just trying to look like a golfer.

Toward the end of the dinner, someone mentioned how much money they had received, about five thousand dollars. I said, "Are you kidding me? I could get five grand in Palm City." I looked around and thought, *There are people in the room worth a hundred million, and a few billionaires. Come on, only five grand for a bunch of wounded guys who are going to do a marathon? Help us out.*

I started looking for Mary. When I found her, I said, "Let me speak. Can you get the mic?"

She said, "You're willing to speak?"

I said, "Yeah, this is bad. Five thousand dollars? With this crowd? It's pathetic." She brought me up on stage. I took the mic and just started talking.

I don't remember what I said, but I do remember looking down and seeing tears running down Jim Palmer's face. I told myself, *Okay, Luke. Maybe a little too real.* I knew I had to build them back up. I talked about the upcoming marathon and said, "You all can look for me at the finish line. Hopefully, I'll be first." Of course, I knew that wasn't true—there were several other guys on our team who could smoke me. But I got that audience fired up. The fundraiser shot up to about sixty-seven thousand dollars in five minutes. That's how it's done.

The Palm Beach experience gave me some confidence. Not for fundraising, because I do not like to fundraise, but knowing that I could win the crowd, because that's what I did. I realized it was important to tell my story. There are so many guys like me who can't, whether they just don't like public speaking or they aren't ready to tell their story. I decided then that I could help give a voice to this new generation of wounded service members.

My second marathon with Achilles was in Pensacola, Florida. I was better trained, but then I went out the night before and partied. I was a bad boy. The other team members and I had gone to this place with a piano bar in one part and a nightclub that was raging in another. I was there with a crew of guys with no legs and wheelchairs, and we started drawing some attention. There are a lot of different military installations over that way. Guys came up and asked if we were in the service, saying they were Navy, Air Force, law enforcement. I think one guy was a warrant officer. Everywhere we went, people were throwing drinks our way.

Next thing you know, I was having a very good time. Everyone else on the Achilles Team went back to the hotel, except me. I met this one military guy who had no legs, and he was wild. I was hanging out with him and figured I'd try to be in around eleven p.m., get five or six hours sleep, drink a bunch of water, and be fine for the race. No big deal. I wasn't going for the gold medal or anything. But somehow, I never made it back to the hotel. When I walked up to the marathon the next morning wearing the same clothes from the night before—polo and jeans—my Army buddies on the team started catcalling and giving me hell. Mary saw me and said, "You'd better get your shirt on right now!" She was so mad. I put on my race jersey, found some shorts, and got on the bike. I was looking for water to keep on the sled with me. When I heard the pistol shot, I went for it. That was a really windy race, which is the worst on a hand-crank bike because you have to work for every little bit of speed you can get. But I finished; I even beat a few of the other guys on our team. And Mary somehow forgave me.

Trips arranged by groups like Achilles that help service members can make a real difference in our lives. Skiing in Snowmass started me back on the right track. And after my first marathon, I realized, *I'm not handicapped at all. I'm still competing, still sweating. I'm still in the game.*

One time, I was invited to be part of a Wounded Warrior Project Soldier Ride from Miami to Key West, a three-day ride that included a stop to swim with the dolphins. There was one kid with us, maybe nineteen years old, who had both his legs blown off by an IED. He didn't smile the whole trip and wouldn't talk much. When we got in the water, one of the dolphins came right up to him and started putting on a show, like he sensed his need. He grabbed onto the fin for a ride, and his face just lit up as the dolphin skidded him across the water—fast. He was going way faster than the rest of us; that dolphin was giving him a little more and we all knew it. His parents saw it, too, and cried. I heard his mom say, "That's the first time he's smiled since he was injured."

Bringing the vets together helps us help each other, too. When we raced a marathon in Miami, I met this guy Andrew who put all of us veterans to shame. He was one of the top guys in the Naval Academy and was allowed to go into the Marine Corps. He was in theater less than a month when he lost both his legs in a blast, up to the hip on one side and really high on the other. Andrew decided to go to Harvard and get his MBA and law degree. There weren't that many guys who wanted to return to college after their injuries. He went all the way, and that's good for the rest of us to see what's possible.

CHAPTER 27

Finding a Future

Shortly after I returned to Florida from Walter Reed, Kristine, the girl I dated for eight years and had become engaged to, told me she wasn't happy, and we broke up. That was probably the most pain that I'd ever felt in my life. She had been part of my purpose for holding on. When I was lying in that pool of blood after the blast, it was her face I pictured at my funeral, along with my Mom. And I fought to stay alive. I didn't want to do that to them. And now she was gone. I fell into a deep place. I might have been smiling on the outside, but deep down I was dead. There were days I didn't want to live. I never went for help, I didn't talk to therapists. I never got deep into booze or did drugs to escape the pain. I just toughed it out. Somehow, I survived that blast, too.

* * *

There's this sense of trust you've got to have with your prosthetic leg. I saw a double above-the-knee amputee put a baby on his shoulders and take off walking. Other guys won't let go of the bars in rehab. But you just have to trust.

It starts between your ears, with a mental attitude and toughness. I tell myself, I'm not going to let this beat me. Instead, I focus on the positive things in life. You're at a greater risk of tripping, and so you have to be a lot more cautious. Just yesterday, I tripped and hit the ground. Falling six feet, I could break my arm or wrist, but luckily I didn't. But it's always in the back of my mind. Everything I do is thought out; I don't want any more setbacks.

Other amputees who have seen me walking around have mentioned how well I walk, and they think it's because I have a fancy military leg. Civilians don't get the stuff that we get. But I think a lot of my success as an amputee has been because of the training I received at Walter Reed. Our therapists worked with hundreds of amputees every day, whereas civilians at a regular rehab might get a therapist who sees one every week. Having a more experienced therapist helps. They can adjust their techniques and know what to look for, how to coach you.

Therapists even teach you how to fall. They tell us we're going to fall, so get used to it. Sometimes they'd see us standing by a mat, and they would come push us over. It was practice for the real thing.

These legs are designed to go up and down stairs. And if you stay confident, you can do it. There are things you can do to make yourself better. A lot of it is core strength and balance. I've seen amputees who were way more athletic than me, and I'm walking better than them because I've developed the muscles and balance.

I think back to my childhood. I always looked up to my older brother. He had this inner strength and inner balance, and I try to bring that into my amputee life. Just put my shoulders up, head up and go. Get ready to fall.

* * *

There was this philanthropist in my hometown named John Pierson who owned a Toyota dealership. He was all over the TV promoting his business, and he gave money away to every cause. John supported baseball teams in the county that couldn't get a sponsor, he gave big to the Humane Society and to Beds 4 Babies—he gave to all of them.

Someone told me he owned a house on the Intracoastal Waterway and that he'd combined it with a home next door, then built a hundred-thousand-dollar deck connecting them. He even had a built-in pirate ship bar. He was one of the rich guys that I didn't know, since I was a country boy. My entire life growing up, until I left for the military, I didn't know anyone who owned a beach house. Not one person. Where I'm from, you need a couple of million dollars to have a home on the ocean. The ones who do are mostly part-timers from up north. Martin County is a blend of Yankees, old country boys, and Miami folks, so I didn't know anybody like John.

My mom had gotten to know John and his wife through her massage therapy business. He attended the benefit fundraiser they had for me the year I was injured and wrote a check for five thousand dollars.

After my rehabilitation, when I moved home, I dropped by the Toyota dealership to buy a new truck. I had been driving an F-250 Power Stroke Diesel, but since I wasn't going into the construction business, I didn't need that gas guzzler. Buying from John's dealership was kind of a return gesture for John supporting me.

The next day, I received a call from the dealership. "Would you mind coming back here? John Pierson wants to see you." Apparently, he'd found out about my purchase and was not happy. He's the type who would have wanted to give a wounded guy a better deal.

When I got off the elevator leading to John's personal office, he was standing there dressed in a costume from a 1950s Western, maybe Roy Rogers. I thought, *There's no way I will be able to take this guy seriously.* He explained it was for a commercial shoot and then got right down to business. "I hear you bought a truck."

I said, "Yeah, I wanted to even things out a little bit." He looked at me like, *Who the hell do you think you are?*

We talked a little while, and he said he was having a party the following weekend and invited me. I went, but I didn't try to play the part or pretend I belonged with that crowd; I was just myself. Then John invited me to another party. The next thing I knew, I was on the up-and-comers scene in Martin County. I got invited to speak at Shepherd's Park for Veteran's Day in front of a crowd of a few thousand people. That was one of my biggest speeches ever. I stood on the stage with my state legislator and US congressman. It was only a two-minute speech, but I connected with the audience. People were beginning to know who I was, and it was all because of John.

Kristine and I had broken up by then, so I spent a lot of time at John's house. I was like family. He worked out at the most expensive gym in town and arranged for me to work out with him. His trainer had been Mr. Florida and Mr. World, so I got to work out every day at a gym I couldn't afford with a trainer who cost a hundred dollars an hour. It was great.

John threw a surprise party for me at his home and spent thousands on fireworks. It was April 25, 2009, the third anniversary of the blast. John and I were on a boat and had just pulled up to John's dock when they surprised me. All the big politicians were there, and the business leaders in town, plus my whole family. John kept telling me, "This is your day. This is your day." I said, "What are you talking about?" One of the officials read a proclamation that explained it. They had made April 25 "Luke Murphy Day" in Martin County.

John was always throwing parties. A few months later, at another one, he had an Army helicopter brought in to surprise me. I didn't realize it, but John was grooming me. I'd tell him my ideas about different business ventures that may have been a little farfetched, and he'd set me straight, "No, what about this…?" He was trying to get me out of my small thinking, my country-boy staff-sergeant mentality. I knew

John had gone to Auburn and was an All-American swimmer. By his late twenties, he was making half a million a year. John helped open my eyes to things that were a lot nicer than anything I'd ever seen in my life, and I began thinking of my own future a little differently. I even started working on the way I talked. He got after me about my grammar, and I was almost hurt, but I got the point. I got it.

One night, John said, "Let's have some folks over. Just invite your closest friends." I called about ten friends. There was a beautiful breeze blowing through the palm trees over the pool. We were way up on this bluff looking over the inlet and the ocean. My buddies had never seen anything like it.

John said, "Luke, come walk with me for a minute." We strolled toward the other side of the house, and he said, "Sometimes in life you've got to accept things." I thought he was about to tell me I was a dumb redneck or something. We walked out to the front of his house, away from the water, and there was a big crowd standing there...next to a brand-new, jacked-up black Toyota Tundra with a giant red ribbon around it. That's the truck I still drive today.

As generous as John was, I never saw that one coming. I don't ever expect anything, but people have always been so good to me. Maybe it's because I've been real and I've opened up.

Whenever I talk to John, he says, "I'm proud of you. I love you." That kind of stuff. He tells people I remind him of John Wayne because I've got a little gimp in my walk and a little attitude in my talk. It's funny to hear him say it.

John Pierson was my first major mentor. He really unlocked my potential. He helped me quit thinking of myself as an enlisted guy and realize that these other people who grew up with more than I did don't have anything on me. There's no glass ceiling. He was the first person who told me, "You can do whatever you want."

John was self-made. He earned every penny himself. Not that he doesn't have problems—we all do—but I can learn from those as well. I can learn what not to do. I can learn from anybody, at the top or the bottom. I look at everybody like they have value. But when I'm around somebody smarter or more gifted than me, I'm watching and trying to learn, and I've learned a lot from him.

At twenty-seven, I was dating again, living on the river, and spending a lot of time out on my boat. I was in the news, and it's a small town, so for my age I was a relatively big fish. I ran into an acquaintance I'd known from my teenage years, Louie Frosch. He showed up at my house for a party. One of my best buddies had dated Louie's sister. I knew his dad died when we were teenagers, and from what I understood, he was a pretty tough guy, lived a rough life, and died young. Louie was very smart, but he was also very tough. It's a weird combination. He wasn't tall, but nobody messed with him. My buddies and I took him with us on a few hog hunts in our younger years. We could tell he had a lot of grit, but he referred to books that none of the rest of us had ever read.

I enlisted in the National Guard, and Louie went into the Marine Corps infantry. We'd see each other occasionally at parties. We were usually the only military, so we had a little connection there. After I went active duty, I heard that Louie had a heart rhythm problem, an irregular heartbeat. When the doctors went to fix it, they botched something, and he had to undergo emergency open-heart surgery. They opened up his chest, and it totally messed him up. He had to get out of the Marines, so he decided to go to college and study to be a doctor to make sure those types of things don't happen.

It was the fall of 2008 when we saw each other again, and Louie was premed at Florida State University. I thought it was kind of rare for a twenty-seven-year-old infantry Marine to be in college, and premed at that—with tattoos. He looked around my house and smirked. "Hey, you've got it going on." I told him I was having fun and asked about college. "It's good. You should think about it." I told him I didn't think it was for me. Still, that question lingered in my mind the next day and over the next few weeks. Maybe I *should* think about it.

I drove up to Tallahassee to visit Louie one weekend. He was living at a place called the Colony Club not far from the football stadium. It had a huge pool, beautiful young co-eds everywhere, and the whole place just spoke potential.

When Louie was home again for a visit, I called and he came over. I told him I was interested. He told me right away that he would help me move. We'd always been buddies but not like that, but I accepted the offer. I called my oldest brother, Eddie, and told him I was going back to college, to Florida State University. I could tell he didn't believe me at first, but I convinced him.

I wanted to share the news with John Pierson. When we met, he said he couldn't be more proud of me. I told him he was one of the major reasons I was doing it.

A few weeks later, I got a U-Haul truck and a rental pull-behind, and we loaded Louie's truck on it. We loaded up everything I owned into the U-Haul. I drove my truck with the boat behind it, seven hours to Tallahassee. My buddy, Dave, who owns Deren's Land Surveying in Gainesville came to help and so did my buddy, George Faulk, from Marianna, who served both tours with me. All these military guys helped move me into a one-bedroom apartment at the Colony Club.

Louie kind of became my mentor in college. When I called to ask what he was doing one night and mentioned everything that was going on, he told me he was staying home to study. He added, "I don't go out every night. You can't." It made me realize that maybe I had some studying to do, too. Louie helped impress upon me that what I was doing was important, and I started looking at things differently. I took it more seriously and ended up making A's and B's. Louie was only there for a semester with me, and then he graduated and went off to med school, but he set the tone: get your business done first, and then party.

After Louie left, I didn't know anybody and missed the camaraderie of the military. I met other guys—an Army Ranger and a Marine sniper. But I kept feeling like I was missing the full college experience. I didn't want to reach out and be friends with just any eighteen-year-old. I'd been told about fraternities and how they were the kids that came from good families and the kids who would probably end up going to good jobs, and I thought, *Man, if John Pierson were here, he would tell me to meet those kids and stay friends with them through the years.*

My first summer in college, I was dating this girl and was around her younger brother and some of his friends. I thought for younger guys they were dressed correctly, not punks, and they said they were KAs. I said, "What's a Kappa Alpha?" They said they were a fraternity known around campus as southern gentlemen. That piqued my interest. A guy was at my house that August and told me fraternity rush was going on the next night. I said I'd thought about that, but felt I was too old. He said, "If you did go, you'd probably be a good KA. You're really conservative."

I thought, *I'm only going to college once. I'm here and I don't know anybody. Nobody's judging me. Let's get the full experience.* Sure, I didn't have parents to pay for everything, but I had enough from the Army retirement, plus my school was covered through a benefit I optioned my first year of service. I knew I wasn't going to rage and funnel beers every night, but I could be one of them. I went to the rush party and saw the guys I'd met from summer, and a group of them immediately pulled me aside. They said, "If you want to be one of us, we'd love to have you." I thought I was just showing up to hear a pitch. I was sucked in before I knew it.

But I went for it and pledged. I learned a lot from those young men. I was very impressed. There were eighteen-year-olds who held bible studies, seemed wise, and treated girls right. They were mature, goal oriented, and came from good families. It was a good decision for me.

Since I graduated, the KA alumni have called me to come talk to the guys. I had wanted to tap their connections, but I see now it works both ways. When I got my Homes for Our Troops house, one of the KA alums, Bruce Hagan, spoke at the ceremony, and a bunch of alumni pitched in and bought the furniture for it. I didn't ask for a thing.

Bruce told the audience that a number of my fraternity brothers joined the military and said they would never have thought about it before meeting me. I know many who didn't get DUIs because I was there. The brothers have adopted philanthropies for homeless vets. Somehow, I changed their lives by just being me, maybe putting things in perspective. And they unlocked a lot of doors for me that were previously closed. Influence works both ways.

CHAPTER 28

Hammertoes

My senior year in college, Colonel Steele asked me to come to Atlanta for a skeet-shoot fundraiser to benefit wounded vets. As much as I wanted to say, "Sir, I'm in college. There's not much time to practice shooting skeet, and besides that, I'm not thrilled about driving my truck that gets twelve miles a gallon to Atlanta," I wasn't saying no to the colonel. If Colonel Steele asked me to come in the middle of the night with a shovel, I'd be there. "Yes, sir. All right." So I went.

He and I got to have lunch with former Georgia Bulldogs football coach Vince Dooley. He is basically the Bobby Bowden of Georgia; he's like some people's Jesus. I knew that Colonel Steele played for him when they won the national championship with 1982 Heisman Trophy winner Herschel Walker. I immediately liked Coach Dooley. He was probably in his eighties, but still looked really strong, like he could beat somebody up.

Of course, I told him I was a Florida State Seminole, which is in a different conference so doesn't play Georgia in a regular season. Colonel Steele said, "Oh, you're going to love Colonel McKnight." I said, "Colonel McKnight is a Seminole fan?" He said, "Colonel McKnight went to Florida State." I didn't really know anything about him except he was in the movie *Black Hawk Down*; in fact he was the Third Battalion Ranger commander in Mogadishu, in Somalia. And he was my colonel's boss, when Colonel Steele was Captain Steele. He said I would be meeting McKnight later that day at the awards ceremony. This trip was getting better and better.

Colonel Steele had seen me entertaining some of the guys by turning my fake leg upside down and doing the FSU Seminole "chop" like all the fans do in the stadiums. He thought it would be funny for me to do it in front of everyone during the conclusion ceremony with Colonel McKnight. I thought, *I haven't ever met him, he doesn't know me, and you want me to walk up to him while he's got the mic in his hand, turn my leg around, and start breaking it down? And I'm sober?*

This wasn't the nose chop like most people do, this was like some terrible amputee dance. To me, it was a bad idea, but you can't tell the colonel no. It's just ingrained in you. Late that afternoon, Colonel Steele grabbed the emcee, a retired NFL wide receiver, and told him what I was going to do. I saw him grin real big and motion me over, like, *Yeah, yeah, come on, let's go. It's time.*

I saw McKnight standing under the tent on the country club lawn. He's about average size, maybe five nine, but an infantry officer, so he was a tough SOB. He said, "Ladies and gentlemen, please welcome Staff Sergeant Luke Murphy." As I walked up, the NFL player took the microphone and put his cell phone up to it to start this rap music. McKnight tried to step away, but I grabbed him by the shoulder and I flipped my leg around and I started breaking it down. The colonel laughed so hard, his mouth was about on the floor. He gave me a look like, "Who *is* this guy?" So that's how I met the big colonel.

I guess I made a lasting impression because McKnight later invited me to be the keynote speaker for a Memorial Day gathering at a park in central Florida. It was scorching hot, and I had on my wool uniform and a wool beret. The sun was reflecting off the river and beating right down on me. There were hundreds of people, and I had to talk about the guys who died and the significance of it and what it means to us and this generation. It was a tough speech. We went to the colonel's home later, and he said, "Who wants to get in the pool?"

I was dying in the wool suit and hat, so we changed into bathing suits and jumped in. The colonel likes to tell this story on me. He asked if I wanted a beer, and I said, "Yes, sir." He brought me a Yuengling, and I thought, *Man, that's pretty good.* I was still on a college-student budget. It went down pretty smoothly, so he asked if I wanted another, and I said sure. About the fourth one, he said, "Dammit, this was a bad idea, this guy has got the colonel fetching him beers." He even went to the store to get more, while I was hanging out with his wife, Linda. The best part is that he doesn't mind telling the story himself. That's McKnight.

* * *

When Colonel McKnight saw me move around without my fake leg, he asked why I didn't hop. I told him it hurt too bad because my toes were bent underneath my foot, and I couldn't straighten them. I showed him and he said, "Those are hammertoes. You need to get them fixed."

I explained, "Well, I'm in college now, and even though they hurt pretty bad, I guess I'll just need to suck it up." The next day he contacted this nonprofit that arranges surgeries for veterans at no cost to them. It's not for guys who need something their first year, but for those who need a follow-up.

A lady named Maggie called me as soon as I returned home. She asked if I wanted to get my toes fixed. I said, "If you guys want to do it, what's one more surgery?" I hadn't had a surgery since Walter Reed, and I avoided hospitals. I visited them when people asked, and I would try to be really happy and upbeat. But I didn't stay long. I've spent way too much of my life in hospitals. So anything that wasn't killing me, I would put off as long as I could. But after the colonel said he could get it fixed, I didn't want to act like a sissy. He said, "You need to get it fixed," so I answered, "Yes sir." And it was a good idea.

Maggie called again and said she had researched it and there was a really good surgeon in Tallahassee named Dr. Andrew Borom. She asked what I thought, and I said, "Whatever you think." How would I know? Maggie's group, Rebuilding America's Warriors (formerly Iraq Star), was started to help burn victims, guys who have their faces melted off, who have dozens and dozens of surgeries. They should have the best. The pain they have described to me sounds way worse than what I've been through. A lot of these guys are also missing limbs, so they have both kinds of pain.

Dr. Borom told me later that he was with a patient when one of his assistants told him a plastic surgeon was calling from Los Angeles. He thought, *Yeah, right.* He suspected it was one of his residency buddies playing a prank. He took the call, and it was from one of Maggie's docs.

This LA surgeon said, "We need your help. We need you to fix some hammertoes on a wounded veteran." Colonel McKnight had taken some pictures of my foot, so they forwarded them to Dr. Borom. His office called me almost immediately. "When can you come in?" I met him the next day, and after looking at the foot, he said, "I can take care of this, no problem. I'm sorry you've been walking around on these things. Doesn't it hurt?"

I said, "Yeah."

He said, "But not bad enough to come in?"

I said, "No. I'm in college, too busy having fun." He laughed.

We started talking about my experiences in Iraq. He said, "How high did the pain ever get?"

I said, "Probably five or six." I saw his eyebrows go up. To this day, when Dr. Borom gets somebody who tells him they can't work and their pain is a fifteen, he tells them, "You know, I had this guy once with one leg that was all mangled and the other one that was blown off from Iraq, and he said his pain only got to a six. So this is a fifteen?" He does that to people.

We were originally only going to do two toes, but when I woke up after the surgery, I found he did all four of them. He said, "Yeah, I got in there and figured they needed to be done." He broke the knuckles on my toes and fused them straight. He threaded pins through the toe bones, and they were coming out of the tips of each toe, shiny metal pins that were bent over at the ends, pointing downward. I couldn't feel them, but it looked like it should hurt like hell.

I later introduced Colonel McKnight to Dr. Borom, and now the doc is helping a guy who was hit by two grenades. I've also become good buddies with Dr. Borom. He said he will keep working on my good leg until I die. It gets cold, doesn't have good circulation, and it bleeds a lot. It would be a lot easier to just get it taken off. But Dr. Borom says, "No, no, that thing's fine," and I'm going to keep it as long as I can.

CHAPTER 29
Fish Story

Mary called me a few days after my surgery and said, "Luke, I've got a marathon in Costa Rica in two weeks." I said, "That's great, but I've just had surgery." I told her I had four pins hanging out of my toes.

She said, "Oh, no. One of my guys just backed out, and I need to fill his slot."

I said, "It's in Costa Rica?" I had always wanted to go there. A lot of my buddies had been fishing there, and a few of them surfed there, too. It was going to be hard for me to pass up.

She said, "Yes. But it sounds like there's no way you can do it."

I said, "Let me ask my doctor." When I saw Dr. Borom that week, I asked, "Hey, what do you think of me going to Costa Rica and doing a marathon?"

He looked at me like he couldn't believe I was serious. "A marathon? On what, a bike?" I said, yeah, my hand-crank bike. He asked if my foot was going to bounce around, and I said yes. We talked about the quality of the water in Central America, and he warned, "If you shower down there, you could come back with an infection." He was one hundred percent against me going.

A week and a half later, I was on a plane to Costa Rica. I had never been there before, and I was absolutely going. I wasn't going miss it. When I got off the plane, it was really hot and muggy. It was late August. I was in pretty good shape from college, but I had not been riding my bike as much as I needed to for a marathon.

I ended up rooming with this bald guy who was in a wheelchair. From the waist up, he was in really good shape. Anthony was a Green Beret, a Special Forces guy. We were staying in Tamarindo Beach, right on the Pacific, with tiki huts and amazing food. I was watching the water lap in every eight seconds—just a smooth, small roller. Locals were teaching kids how to surf on the beach. There were big, nice swimming pools everywhere. Of course, I couldn't get in the water because of the pins hanging out of my toes. I had this huge boot on and was walking around with a cane. It was so hot and I thought, *This is not a good way to come to Costa Rica.*

Anthony and I got the bikes out and took a little lap just to get used to the road. There were potholes everywhere, and every time I hit one, it jarred my leg, killing my foot. Anthony had a nice bike that was a lot lighter than mine. I thought, *Oh, this guy's going to kill me.*

The night before the race, we turned in at a decent time, then somebody knocked on our hotel room door around midnight. Anthony got in his chair and wheeled over. It was these two drunk girls from Memphis. I'm thinking, *We've got a marathon in the morning, get them out of here.* But he went to swim with them in the pool, so I followed and hung out on the side. I was finally able to talk Anthony back into his chair about two in the morning, and we went back to bed.

We both pounded Gatorades the next day. We weren't talking as much because we were about to race a marathon, and you know, somebody's going to have to lose. There were eight other guys riding hand cranks, five of us from Mary's group, and the rest came from other parts of Costa Rica. They heard about the Achilles Freedom Team, and Mary was going to see if she could get them some bikes to train on—not from Achilles but from a different group that could get them for the disabled who wanted to stay in shape.

Even though it was early in the morning, it was already hot out-side, sticky and nasty. Our shirts were green cotton—bad choice. It was going to be 26.2 miles of potholes, so I put a pillow on my left footrest and wrapped my boot in it, with the pins sticking out. I got the people helping us to tape my leg onto the bike. I was committed. Someone from the hotel came up and said, "You've got a message at the front counter." Since I was strapped in, I told them I'd have to get it when I finished.

They put the hand cranks at the front of the starting line because we blow out of the gates a lot faster than runners. When we heard the pistol shot, we took off. There's no pacing in hand cycling. You go all out the whole way, or at least you try. Within no time, I was up at the very front. I looked over my shoulder a few times just to see where everybody was. I could see Anthony. He wasn't far behind. I kept it up until I felt it was starting to get a little much and backed off a little, and there he was. We were zipping through the countryside of Costa Rica. Villages, really poor folks. We went by a cemetery, and it smelled like somebody wasn't buried deep enough. Anthony looked at me, and we both knew exactly what it was. Every bump was lighting up my leg. The pins were dancing around my toes. I didn't have skin feeling, but the rest felt like someone was digging a knife around the inside of my leg and into my foot as well.

Anthony would go in front, then I would. When we got to the top of the turnaround point, I poured it on again. If you've ever done mil-itary long runs at a fast pace and you're leading the group in a forma-tion, you'll see guys look up once in a while like, *When is he going to stop?* Your eyes meet, and you take it up another notch. Then they'll just quit—it's a mental beatdown.

I'd used that trick for years in the infantry, so I thought I had this guy. I got a pretty good lead on him and thought, *Yup, it worked*. I didn't think I'd have to keep that pace; he was just going to think I had more and more. But after a while, I felt him coming up on me. *Dammit.* Then he was right behind me, he was drafting me.

My entire marathon career had been a matter of being in decent shape, maybe riding once a week, having a good time the night before a race and killing the body the next day with whatever God-given talent I had. It was nothing compared to what this guy was doing, riding about a hundred miles a week. But I was still in the lead and thought, *I got him, I got him.* We got to mile twenty, then twenty-four—we had been at it for more than an hour and a half. We got to the last mile, twenty-six, and I thought, *I'm going to get him now.* There was no way he had anything left. If I made him think I was just going to turn up this speed all the way, he'd quit. So I did it, and it worked for thirty or forty yards, and then I couldn't hold it any longer. Anthony started slowly gaining, and I thought, *Uh-oh, peaked too early.* He was coming up on the side of me, and I could see the crowd. I could see the finish line. In my mind, I'm having a conversation with myself. This is where you dig deep, you go down to that bottom spot of your gut and you just pull it out from somewhere and you just make it happen.

If you've ever caught an interception, this was that moment. I saw all the people, I heard them yelling. I could see the huge timer. I saw Anthony beside me in my peripheral vision, but I wasn't looking back. I had to win. He was slowly gaining on me. I could see him. I saw both of our front tires, and he inched ahead. I told myself, *All right, you've got to get him now. This is it.* I couldn't, though, I was spent. We crossed the finish line, and he beat me by a tire. I was so mad. I honestly wanted to wheel over and punch him in the face. I was so angry that I hadn't had anything left. That lasted for about forty-five seconds. I was trying to catch my breath, and I knew what I needed to do. I cooled down, then went over and gave Anthony a high five.

This was a destination marathon, so people were celebrating like crazy afterward. I received a small clay pot that said, Second Lugar, which means second place. I even won two hundred dollars. I got my first massage on the beach, and it was really cool, even though I had this stupid boot on, my foot hurt like hell, and I just got beat. It was the closest I had ever gotten to winning. I led the thing and couldn't get it done.

After showering, I remembered that message, so I went back to the front desk. I was told, "Call this number." I thought it was weird; I didn't know anybody in Costa Rica. When I called it, I heard this older man answer. He was a boat captain and said, "I don't know who you are, boy, but somebody from Tallahassee bought you a marlin fishing trip." A family I had gotten to know while in school at Florida State knew I was going to be in Costa Rica, so they arranged for me and any of my buddies to go blue marlin fishing the next day.

I went back and asked that joker who had beat me, and some of the other guys, "You want to go marlin fishing in the morning?" They had been looking for things to do and saw the prices, so no way any of us could even think about going deep-sea fishing. They couldn't believe it.

Anthony was in his chair, so the next morning, they put him on a small boat, ran him through the surf, then got him onto the big boat, then they came and got the rest of us and ran us through the big waves. The captain was a white-haired, deep-tanned expatriate who was very stern and professional. He gave us the rules of the boat ride, which is important to military guys. We knew not to screw around. Once we were heading out, he said that the economy had been so bad this was the first time he'd been out all year. Not many boats had been out for marlin; they were doing the in-shore fishing, instead. I looked out over the water and saw a tree the size of a school bus floating. I thought, *I've never seen that in the Atlantic.* It was so big, like Jack and the Beanstalk size, probably a banyan tree. I had never been in this ocean before or seen it, touched it, smelled it. Now I was seeing big-ass trees on it while going to get a blue marlin.

Since the captain hadn't been out, he told us honestly he didn't know where to go for the bites. But he'd been fishing the area for thirty-five years, so he could take a guess. The mates hadn't fished a lot that year, either. Marlin fishing is a calculated process. You had teasers out, a sport-fishing rod and a very light drag. You're watching for a black spot to come behind the bait and tease it with his beak, that long bill. That's your cue to grab the pole, point it at the fish, and dump the bail, but you've got to keep your finger on it, or it'll backlash, and you'll ruin the whole thing. Timing is critical. When the fish sees the bait fall back, it triggers an instinct to bite. Marlin might swim behind the bait all day without biting, unless you drop it back and make it look natural. You've got to feed it and then slowly advance the drag and set the hook. You don't want to jerk it out of the marlin's mouth; you need to set that hook right. It's a very delicate balance. I've done it many times for sailfish out of Stuart, Florida, but never in the Pacific. I wasn't about to act like I knew anything. I just sat back, kept my mouth shut, and did what I was told.

A black spot emerged behind the boat, and we all started freaking out. Captain suddenly had a different energy in his voice. A young Costa Rican ran over and grabbed the pole to feed it. That looked right to me, but I heard the captain yell, "No! No! No!" Sure enough, no fish on the pole. The captain turned the boat viciously to the left. He didn't care where any of the lines were at this point, and he started cranking on the shotgun, which is the pole way off the back of the boat. It was a little rod, not for catching marlin. He started flying that thing in, reeling as fast as he could and steering the boat in a hard circle at the same time. He walked that bait right in front of the marlin's face. He ate it and captain set the hook. This old salt just brilliantly set it. Then he passed the pole with the fish on it down from the tower to one of the mates, who then instructed me to get in the fighting chair. He handed me the rod.

The first thing I noticed was that the rod was way too small to have a marlin on the end of it. And I like to have a larger reel, like a Shimano TL50, to be playing with a marlin—that's the gear you need. This was a Tiagra 20, only there in case the captain saw a sailfish or dolphin. It was probably the worst rod to have for this size of a fish. On top of that, my hands were still very bruised from the marathon, and I wasn't feeling very well.

But I started wrestling with that sucker, and my buddies were slapping me on the back, they were so happy to be part of it. One was filming me fighting the fish, which took a very long time. Eventually, I got the thing all the way to the boat by myself. He was about thirteen feet long, probably 350 pounds. My left foot was shaking, quivering. I'd never caught a fish that big, that strong. I felt agonizing pain around the pins in my foot, my hands were aching from the metal handles of the bike, and my arms, already tired from the day before, were dead again. But I didn't want to pass that rod off. I wanted to catch that fish and get ego credit for bringing in a marlin. I did. I brought him up to the boat, and one of the mates put his hand on its bill and took the hook out. They dragged it along to make sure it was going to be strong, and the fish finally pulled away and dove real deep. It was fine.

As much fun as that experience was, I don't want to ever catch a fish that big again. I've caught big tuna, fifty-pound yellowfins that kicked my butt. When I hear people say they want to catch a marlin, I'm happy for them, but I'm done with the big boys. You've got to have legs and a back for that fish. Pulling with your arms and leg with no calf and no hamstring and all your toes with pins in them is not a good idea. Even though it was pretty incredible.

Anthony had been laughing the whole time I was fighting. He had a huge grin at the end. When it was his turn, he got one and started the fight, but it came off, unfortunately.

After the marlins, we went deep dropping with electric reels. We caught some gorgeous deep-water snapper and grouper, pulling them up slowly from easily five hundred feet of water. One fish looked like a monkfish, but it had a solid tail. We brought our catch to a restaurant later in the day. We paid them fourteen dollars, and they cooked all this fish—boiled, baked, and fried—then served it to us with plantains and rice. They cooked it like nobody's business, adding sauces and toppings. We ate like the locals.

CHAPTER 30
More Than a Project

While I was at Walter Reed, I kept seeing these black backpacks with a Wounded Warrior Project logo hanging on wheelchairs. A guy named R.J. Meade would go room to room, joke around with us, and hand out the packs. They were filled with socks and underwear, things we didn't have at the hospital. He also had some pink Wounded Warrior shirts to give our girlfriends or wives. That's the first time I'd heard of the organization, when they were about three years old and only had a few thousand in the bank.

A bunch of us were invited to the Japanese ambassador's house in DC. They provided entertainment, and the food was incredible. The ambassador's Secret Service guys all looked like Dan Nguyen. They wore dark suits, and when they came into our hospital rooms, they would bow in greeting. They were very respectful and loved fellow warriors. The compound in DC had koi ponds, ten acres of awesomeness. I was sitting in my wheelchair, and I saw a young captain in dress blues, an amputee below the knee, and he was wearing a purple heart. I'm an enlisted so I've never hung out with officers; it wasn't allowed. He came up to me and said, "How are you doing, staff sergeant?" I answered formally. "Fine." I was cordial, but my active-duty mindset told me I didn't have much to say to an officer, so that was the end of our conversation.

A year later, I started seeing the Wounded Warrior Project on TV, and they were doing a lot more for us. They weren't helping me personally at the time; it's not like they've got this master list with fifty thousand people on it that they can get to all at once. If you want help, you've got to ask for it, you've got to start the dialogue. Maybe call and tell them, "Hey, I like to hunt," or "I need some help getting back to school." Then you're on their radar. We get out of the military, change our phone number, and we're hard to find.

When I returned to Florida and started college, the WWP invited me to a turkey hunt, and I saw that same captain from the ambassador's house. He introduced himself as Jonathan Pruden, and I said "Yeah, I know you." I told him where we met, what he was wearing and where we were standing. He acted surprised how much I remembered. We started talking, and that's when I learned that he had been one of the first IED victims in 2003.

Pruden invited me to another event, and we became friends, staying in touch while I was at FSU. He received a master's degree from the University of Florida in Gainesville, so I give him hell about the Gators—the Seminoles' biggest rival. One day he called and said, "Hey, you want to go on a fishing trip?"

My answer: "Where and when?"

He told me, "Tomorrow morning, out of Fort Lauderdale." It was an eight-hour drive, but I wasn't going to miss it. "See you tonight."

When I arrived, I found out that another warrior had backed out, opening up the spot for me. A good thing, because we were going out on Jimmy Buffett's boat, and we were the first group allowed on it. The captain, Vinnie LaSorsa, has a brother who is a Marine. He wanted to do something for wounded vets, so he contacted the WWP. The boat we went out on is manufactured by Rybovich, and they call the model the Margaritavitch. Buffet named his *The Last Mango*. We caught blackfin tuna, dolphinfish (mahimahi), and a yellowfin tuna that day. You generally have to go to the Bahamas to catch yellowfin, and when we got back to the docks, someone saw the catch and asked if we had a nice trip "across," meaning to the Bahamas. Vinnie was a little offended, but I didn't care. What a great trip. Vinnie and I became friends, and he's taken out dozens of groups since then.

Even though Pruden has moved through the ranks as WWP has grown, he has stayed accessible. He has his hands full because he covers the Southeast, and there are a lot of military bases in Florida and a really high concentration of us in Georgia, too. But when I meet other guys who need something, he's always willing to help. I can still make that one phone call and get things done quickly.

After I participated in a few of the WWP's soldier rides and fishing and hunting trips, WWP invited me to be on their National Campaign Team. Since then, I've been featured in their commercials and on fliers, and some of our faces are on Brawny paper-towel wrappers. NCT members share their stories to raise awareness for the most recently injured servicemen and women, and serve as examples of how to live an active life after injury. They're a good organization.

* * *

In 2010, the Wounded Warrior Project asked me to go to Europe with a group of other service members to help raise awareness. We met twenty-five wounded Brits and hand cycled all over Europe. I got to see major World War I and World War II battle sites. I learned so much history by seeing it firsthand. I went where my grandpa and great uncle went when they served. I went to the national graveyards and saw thousands of white crosses. I saw Patton's grave. I saw the beaches in Normandy, and I felt that wind barreling off the coast and saw how angry the ocean was, and I saw the pillboxes full of machine guns that the Americans had to charge. They had their hands full. It helped put my war in perspective. My war was deadly, I almost died, but I didn't have to charge a beach, and I never scaled a cliff. I did everything I was asked and then some, but I felt so damned honored to see where these service members fought, and imagined how they did it. It made me feel a little less sorry for myself and my struggle.

On the trip, I met a double amputee named Kevin Pannell. He was hurt in Sadr City like me, hit by two grenades, and he saw the guy who threw them. One day Kevin told me he lived in a house built by Homes for Our Troops. These are disabled-accessible homes that are designed around your particular needs. He said, "They're building homes for guys like you now." I'd heard about the group back at Walter Reed, but a physical therapist had told me they were for double amputees only, so I put it out of my mind. I thought, *I'm not hurt bad enough? No problem, help out the ones who are, and I can take care of myself.* That has always been my attitude. But if an organization could do something for me, I'd absolutely appreciate it. At the time, they couldn't.

I was about to graduate from college, and I had the world ahead of me, so my first reaction was *I don't need it, I'm good.* Then Kevin said, "Man, I'll be honest with you, it's the best thing that's ever happened to me. I love my house." And he described all the features in it that made it easier for his regular routine—cooking, cleaning, bathing. Then on the trip, I picked up on more things about his house that sounded so nice, just functional.

When I returned home, I filled out an application. They called me about a week later and said they normally don't build homes for guys like me, but due to the severity of my injuries, I would be strongly considered. I would be way down the list, because there were guys hurt much worse than me, which meant it could be a few years. I said, "I understand. Thank you so much." It would be like winning the lottery.

They asked me to write a letter saying why I thought I should be a recipient, since I was only an AK, a single above-the-knee amputee.

I started the letter by describing my injuries, how they go beyond the above-the-knee amputation. So many of my surgeries have been on my left leg, the good one.

I knew at the time that the president of the board of directors for Homes for Our Troops was General Richard Cody, a four-star general and a 101st guy. He came and saw me at Walter Reed. He sat down—a four-star general visiting with a staff sergeant—and we talked a lot. He told me about a time when he left his base on a ruck march to practice. He was wearing a short shirt, his boots, and a big, heavy backpack. He didn't know it, but the guards were told not to let anyone in after a certain hour. When General Cody returned to the base, some private wouldn't let him in the gates. He was trying to tell the kid who he was, and the private said, "Yeah, right." General Cody called the kid's officer, and that's when the privates at the gate realized this really was the commander. They thought they were going to get killed. We laughed about it—his situation and theirs.

I had another connection to General Cody. My unit was coming home in September 2006, five months after the blast. That would have been the end of the tour for me, too. One of my recovery goals was to be standing there when my guys got off the plane. My surgeons told me point blank, "There's no way, Luke. You just can't be up and moving that fast." It was mainly my good leg that was the problem.

I told them, "I've got to do it. It means a lot to me." I kept reminding the doctors as the date got closer, but they were not optimistic, and my bones weren't cooperating, either. Somehow, I made it. I was really weak, sick, and on so many drugs to hold down infection and manage the pain. At that point in my recovery, I was doing good if I could get nine hours out of a day. The rest were spent pale and nauseous or sleeping. But I got on a plane and flew to Fort Campbell with my dad.

We went out to the hangar, the same hangar where I returned from Iraq in 2004. It was strange to see it from the civilians' perspective. I quickly found some Army guys and crutched over to them. I had the external fixator on my left leg—the cage—and was missing half of my right leg. I told them, "Hey, I'm Staff Sergeant Murphy. I was injured during deployment, and these are my guys. I want to be out there when they come in."

One of them, a lieutenant colonel, said, "Absolutely not. Nobody's on the flight line except for the ones who have been cleared, the ones who are on this list," and he pointed to a clipboard.

I shrugged. "Well, I'm going out there."

He stiffened. "You're not going anywhere."

I spotted General Cody in the crowd, and my dad said, "Let's go get him." He'd met General Cody at Walter Reed and really liked the guy, too. So I crutched over and greeted him, "General Cody."

He recognized me. "Murphy!"

I didn't waste any time. "Sir, I want to be out on the flight line when my men come in. That's been my goal this whole time."

He said, "All right. We'll make it happen." General Cody had no business with the 101st, he had no jurisdiction, and he was just in from Washington. One of his sons was a helicopter pilot, and he was there to see him arrive home. Cody had been in Iraq during our tour, so I'm sure he wanted to see our guys in, too.

The plane touched down, and I heard the families cheering, and some women were sobbing. Kids were crying and laughing. My dad and I were standing off to the side, and in front of us was this big area leading up to the hangar that was taped off. Maybe twenty people were standing there, arms crossed, waiting. I knew the guys would come off the plane, march in, sing a few songs, and then be released to their families. As the plane was taxiing in, I started to lift the tape, and that POAG lieutenant colonel with a clipboard stopped me.

Even though a staff sergeant has no business taking on a lieutenant colonel, I was blown up and figured he couldn't do anything to me, so I kept moving forward. "I'm going out there." I was balancing on my crutches, my left leg was leaking blood, and I was dizzy. But I wanted to be out there, I wanted to see my guys before they saw their families. I knew I wouldn't be able to see them after that because they'd be off in different directions. As I inched forward, the guy grabbed me by the shirt to physically restrain me.

I heard General Cody's voice over my shoulder. "What's the problem?"

The guy released me and pointed to the clipboard. "I've got a list, sir, and he's not authorized to be out here."

General Cody pointed at his four stars and said, "I authorized it—I authorized it!"

The lieutenant colonel backed up and said, "Yes, sir."

General Cody held up the tape for me, and we walked up toward the hangar together. It was about a hundred-yard walk, and I couldn't do forty feet in therapy. But I was able to make it there before the plane came to a stop.

When the doors opened, the colonel and first sergeants came off first, and they looked out. I saw their eyes light up when they saw me below. They came right down, hugged me, and shook my hand. They had to stay composed because they still had to march everybody in. I could tell I had pretty much screwed up their plan.

As my guys came off the plane, one of them shouted my name. They came down and were hanging on me, hugging me and about to knock me over. It was a good moment. I was on air crutching back with them toward their families. I almost fell once, but a few of them caught me and put me back up.

They lined up and sang their songs, then rushed over to their families. A few of them came back over to see me again, and I promised I'd hang around a few days to see them. I got to see Roberts and Jefferson on that same trip. It was the first time we'd been together since they left Landstuhl (without my permission). We even went out for a beer one night.

In my letter to Homes for Our Troops, I told that story. I said, "I lost my right leg, and my left leg was blown apart, and I had to fight to keep it. I'm still having surgeries. When my guys came home, I wanted to be out there, and somebody told me no, and General Cody stood up for me. He made it happen. I hope that he's reading this letter, and I'm hoping he'll stand up for me again." I knew he would remember.

Two weeks later, I was in Boston giving a speech for Volunteers of America. I sat with then-US Senator Scott Brown, who had been a colonel in the Army. Homes for Our Troops is also based in the Boston area, so someone must have noticed when the VOA posted a picture of me and the senator together on Facebook. We received eighty-four thousand likes within two hours.

I was on my way back to Florida, on the first leg of the trip, flying through Atlanta. My phone rang, and it was a representative from Homes for Our Troops. He said one of their recipients backed out of the next conference, and he asked if I wanted the spot. They hold these sessions once a quarter in Boston. They bring eight guys in and tell them about the process, and if you're willing, you sign an agreement and you're in. I said, "Are you kidding me? I went from a maybe in a few years to a maybe in two weeks? I am there!"

I returned to Boston two weeks later and kept asking, "Is this for real? Am I guaranteed?" They said, "Luke, we aren't supposed to say anything, but yes, you're guaranteed." At thirty, I was one of the oldest injured there. Several were in their early twenties. Everyone except me was a double or triple amputee, but they were still tough, they didn't complain. I felt very, very lucky to be included. I wanted to say, *Sorry I'm not missing as much as you guys, and I love y'all. I'm just so glad I'm here.*

Eighteen months later, I was moving into my new home. I couldn't believe it.

Before the house, my life was fine. I loved my life after being hurt. I found other things to think about, I found goals to work toward. I never went backward, but now that I've been in the house for more than a year, I can say it's the best thing that ever happened to me. If Homes for Our Troops had not given it to me, I'd still be the guy I am, but this is the most comfortable place I have on the planet.

My dad sold my family home two weeks before I got blown up, so for the first six years after my injury, I had nowhere to go that was handicapped accessible. In college, I lived in a one-bedroom apartment my first year. I had the same rigors as every other student, scaling hills across campus, navigating steep steps going into buildings, trying to get to class on time. I just had an added physical challenge, and it was just as challenging at the apartment. Still, I thought, *This is life, don't complain.*

I never expected to get helped out at such a high level. I told friends of mine that I'd won the lottery, and they said, "You won the lottery? How much did you win?" I told them I didn't *really* win the lottery, but I got a house. It's been overwhelming.

One of the first things I do when I get home is take the prosthetic off and use the wheelchair. You're not supposed to wear the fake leg too long, even though I push mine longer than most. So having a wheelchair-friendly design makes my homelife more relaxing. When I have to travel, I miss it. I miss being able to wheel into my shower, being able to move around without carpet. I'm so comfortable here. It's the greatest thing that ever happened to me.

There is nothing better you can do for a vet who is hurt as bad as me than give them a place where they can be comfortable. Nothing can come close to what these homes have done for my buddy, Neil, who lost both legs, and Kevin, who lost both legs. This is a game changer. The next best thing you could do is find out what a vet enjoys doing and help them reach a goal. Try to help them get out of their slump and motivate them, but that takes some personal involvement and time invested to build trust.

When HFOT invited me to become an ambassador for them, kind of telling my story like I do for Wounded Warriors, I said "Yes, absolutely," even though I'm not sure I'll ever be able to put it into words how much it really means.

CHAPTER 31

What Lasts

It's taken a lot to put me back together. And I'm not sure I'll ever get used to being on the receiving end of things.

It can be tough for soldiers returning. Everybody will tell you, "You're an awesome guy. You've got this great personality," and act like everything's going to fall into place for you. But deep down, we're in a lot of pain. I was in a lot of pain every day. It's not like we have an advantage, either. No employers rushed out to hire *me* after college, even though my GPA was flawless. I had seven years in the military and not a bad mark anywhere. So I know that frustration, I can see why guys go astray. I can understand why they abuse alcohol and drugs. I can understand why they push everyone away and don't want to talk. I've lived it.

One percent of Americans serve this country. One percent. And probably about one percent of them are hurt as bad as I was. I wonder what percentage of Americans actually help guys like us—give us jobs, give us a leg up, help us get our lives back together. Guys who put it all on the line. I bet it's probably one percent.

I hope to help change that percentage because I know that having people help me has made a difference in my quality of life and given me hope. While I was in college, I helped organize a fundraiser for homeless veterans. I got the idea after I met this older man sitting next to me at the VA. I had asked him where he lived. He said, "Oh, I'm homeless." I asked where he stayed, and he told me about a place run by the Volunteers of America. I almost didn't believe him until I went and visited. He and a number of other veterans were homeless, but they had this transitional housing to help while they were reintegrating into society.

My fraternity president and I went to meet with Sean, the guy in charge, who told us he had a ninety percent success rate getting homeless vets into permanent housing. We asked what we could do to help. He suggested volunteering. Instead, we held a barbecue at the American Legion Post 13. We got all the food donated and had a guest speaker, my friend Colonel Danny McKnight. I went around town, got on the radio, got on TV. We ended up raising eight thousand dollars for those vets. I still try to help in any way possible.

It's tough. A lot of guys don't want to talk about what they went through. And there's no way I can include what all I saw in this book. But I think it's important to tell you at least a little bit and maybe make it a little clearer why our veterans are in such a dark place. I feel like I've had a positive outcome from this, because early on I took responsibility. I realized it was *me* in that puddle of blood. I never thought it would be. But it was *me* in that hospital bed. I had to ask myself, *What are you going to do about it?* I decided to try to make the most of it every day. That's what I've done ever since. I try to help every person that I can. But it starts with taking responsibility. It's one thing to say you support the troops, and it's another thing to show it. A lot of these organizations I've been a part of, like the VOA, show it.

* * *

Assistance comes to us veterans in the most unexpected ways. We're not easy to help because it goes against our training. You've got to be tough to survive in combat. I had my first big lesson on how to receive from medical personnel, especially the physicians and nurses. Before I got blown up, I didn't really have any connections to doctors. I'd have to be really sick to go to the doctor; my family just couldn't afford it. Maybe if you're half-dead, you'd go, but otherwise there just wasn't a reason.

After the blast, I felt really vulnerable knowing how much I relied on doctors. How well my doctor performed would determine my quality of life. And it's not like I got to choose that person, either. I am completely at the mercy of the military to provide medical care for me, the same system that got me involved in the war in the first place. And I've got to believe that the doctor they give me is *the* guy.

So far, they have been. And I've been fortunate to have built a relationship with the ones who performed my major surgeries. They've developed an interest and sincerely want to help. I admire how long these surgeons went to school to become MDs. I've never been a school person, so I'm in awe that someone would choose to go for that long. It's way too much school to be about the money, so I think it's genuinely about helping people and healing them. I get that sense when I'm with a good doctor, that they are going to put their hands on me and figure it out and get the job done. And they care. They're not just going to experiment, to rifle through things.

My first orthopedic surgeon at Walter Reed was Dr. Gajewski. He's a big guy, maybe six four, and looks like a giant when you're in a wheelchair. He's nice, kind of a goofball, and he has a good bedside manner. He's not a prima donna or arrogant surgeon; he'll get down on his knee and talk with you.

Dr. Gajewski worked on my stump three times at Walter Reed before they closed it up. That's the last thing, when it's finally stitched up—that's for life. Unless you have a bone infection like I did, then they have to open you back up and compromise the whole area again.

In the summer of 2010, I was studying abroad in Spain for six weeks and had rubbed my skin raw walking and trying to keep up with the other students. We were constantly going up and down stairs; I had to navigate cobblestone streets and climb hills. The teacher had been nervous about letting me go on the trip anyway, so I was trying to tough it out. But my stump was beginning to bleed, and I didn't want to break it down any further, especially because I wasn't in the States. I Facebooked Dr. Gajewski out of desperation. He answered almost immediately and told me exactly where to go, what to buy, and how to fix it. And he sent me pictures on the phone. I was able to go to the market, get what I needed, and take care of the problem. When I messaged him back to say it worked, he wrote, "Don't ever hesitate to call me."

I think most guys who've had Dr. G as a doctor feel they received special treatment. When I was doing a marathon in England, I met a soldier who said he was fortunate to have this very experienced American doctor. He said, "It was a weird Polish name, like Gerguski."

I knew exactly who he was talking about. I said, "Gajewski."

He replied, "Yeah! Big guy!"

Most recently, in the fall of 2014, I was having a lot of pain in my amputated limb and started corresponding with him to ask if he could help. I had not seen him in eight years, and he was now the chief of the Center for the Intrepid at the Brooke Army Medical Center in San Antonio, Texas. We just picked up right where we left off. We had always joked around a lot, but I knew if I wanted to get serious and talk about what was going on, he'd get serious and try to figure it out.

The truth is, I could have probably gotten the surgery done a lot faster if I had gone to the VA hospital in Florida, but this is Gajewski. He's like the Michelangelo of amputation. He wouldn't tell you this, but he's probably done more amputations than anybody else in the world. That's because he spent ten years at Walter Reed; he sees a lot of us blast-wound guys.

When I've had other local doctors do surgeries, Dr. G has consulted with them. He's gotten to know my local surgeon, Dr. Andrew Borom, who did my toe surgery, and that's reassuring for me as the patient.

I realize I never would have enjoyed these types of relationships if I hadn't suffered a catastrophic injury, so it's bittersweet. I've got two really good surgeons, and it's only because of what happened to me. Then I think, *Yes, this bad thing happened and opened the door, but there have been some really great things that have followed.* I think it's because I've had a good attitude, and people appreciate it, instead of the doctors hacking on me and never wanting to see my face again. They seem to want to help forever. Those are the words they use: *The rest of your life.*

* * *

I respect people who sacrifice so much time to help others, like doctors and other medical personnel. In fact, my fiancée is an intensive care unit nurse at one of our local hospitals.

Yes, the guy finally got the girl.

Stephanie and I first met on a hot September day when I was up visiting my friend, Louie, at FSU. I still wasn't sure I wanted go back to college at twenty-seven, so I was just looking around, taking it all in, no pressure. I went out to the pool, took off my prosthetic leg, and jumped in.

This girl Louie told me about from my hometown was walking by the deck chairs with a friend. I said, "Hey, aren't you from Stuart?" Michelle turned around, and she asked how I knew that. I told her I knew Louie. Michelle introduced me to her roommate, Stephanie, who was tan and athletic looking. She had blondish-brown hair pulled back in a ponytail, and she smiled with her eyes.

The next day, I was walking across the parking lot of the complex and saw Stephanie come whipping around the corner behind the wheel of a little brown truck with an orange University of Tennessee sticker on the back. She got out, and I noticed she was wearing blue denim shorts, a T-shirt, and camouflage hat. I thought, *What a cute little country girl.* It was a game day, so Louie and I were loading up my truck with coolers for our tailgate party. We had some time to kill waiting for our buddies, so we started a game of cornhole. It's basically a lawn game where you toss beanbags, trying to get them in a hole. Stephanie came out of her apartment and said hello to Louie as I was tossing. She gave me a hard time because every time I threw, I held my hand in a number-one position. I could tell she was young, and she mentioned a boyfriend. That curbed my interest—I don't make a point to find other guys' girlfriends attractive. We remained friends, though.

When I moved up to go to school, I'd see her around the complex. She was a pole vaulter for the FSU track team and stayed pretty busy, but occasionally she'd go Jeep riding with me and Louie and even showed us some old dirt roads north of Tallahassee. We also had similar taste in music. When I was looking for a home to buy to get out of the apartment, Stephanie came along with me and Louie. She invited me out to have pizza with her parents, and I saw how much she loved her sister and brother and how much they loved her. In my mind, she was a very complete girl.

In 2010, I heard Stephanie and her boyfriend had broken up, and I kind of started looking at her differently. One weekend I invited her to come up to the mountains with me, where I had a piece of property with waterfalls on it. I liked her a lot by then, we'd become closer friends, but she was still playing hard to get. She was not an easy catch.

Stephanie graduated from FSU in the spring of 2011, and I graduated that fall. I really liked Tallahassee and didn't want to leave. By that time I was living in a four-bedroom house with a pool and had roommates. Stephanie had started nursing school, and whenever she wasn't studying, she was right there with us. We spent more and more time together, and when I had one of my surgeries, I guess you could say she became my permanent nurse.

As I was writing the final chapter of this book, I asked Stephanie to marry me. She said yes.

EPILOGUE

When I'm traveling around doing speaking engagements, people often ask me about the guys who were in the blast with me. What ever happened to them?

Erik Roberts, who was sitting in the back left seat, was hit with one round in his thigh, causing a huge laceration and compound fracture to his femur. During his recovery, he had a few setbacks, including pseudomonas like I had, but he managed to pull through. He just ran the Marine Corps marathon and is training for a Half Ironman. Roberts also received a degree in finance from Youngstown State. He called me in early 2014 and asked if I knew anything about the Wall Street Warfighters program, which helps wounded veterans get their Series 6 and Series 7 licenses to become stockbrokers. I happened to know a couple of guys in it, so I put them in touch. Roberts has since nailed his Series 7 and Series 6 licenses and is well on his way to being an investment advisor. He's also a loving dad to his seven-year-old daughter. Roberts is an absolute success—he was blasted by adversity but started setting goals and has healed both physically and mentally. He's been shot at, blown up, and bounced back. He's happy and not bitter. That's miraculous. It's probably because of all that praying he was doing in the triage tent.

Adam Jefferson, who we call AJ, was our gunner that day. The blast caused a compound fracture to his leg. Like Roberts, AJ has made a lot of good decisions and moved on with his life. He's currently working with one of the top private security companies in Afghanistan. That was a goal of his, and he had to go back to the trenches, back to washing clothes in a bucket, to move up in the organization. He did what it takes and is now reaping the rewards. This is the type of company that takes ex-Navy Seals and Green Berets. AJ was trained as a 19 Delta and found himself in the infantry, but I would put him against anybody. He's still serving, still protecting with the best of the best, even though he's no longer in the military. When AJ's not defending people, he's enjoying his life. He's an elite bass fisherman and competes regularly in tournaments.

Shane Irwin was our driver. He was not injured in the blast, but he helped save our lives. And it had to be very difficult on him mentally. While AJ, Roberts, and I got medevaced out of there, he had to stay in theater and go right back to soldiering the next day. I've been in that position, after Jenkins's death, and it's hard. But he stayed. In fact, Irwin is still in the Army. He was promoted to staff sergeant and is a squad leader. He's putting his combat experience to work leading soldiers.

I sometimes wonder about Troy Jenkins's survivors. When Jenkins was blown up, he was married with two sons. One was four and the other two. Most of us never get to meet the families of our fellow service members who pass away. They don't want to see us; it's too painful for them. But in the end, I think it hurts us because we don't get closure. If I did get a chance to meet them, I'd want to tell them how their sons, husbands, and fathers fell and how they were brave, how they didn't just roll over. They fought and they fought hard for their lives. I would want them to know that I am truly sorry for their loss.

* * *

I've done my best to deal with the adversity, too. I've moved on. My new career came unexpectedly. After one of my talks for the Wounded Warrior Project, I received a call from someone who had picked up a check from a local business for us, and he asked how to get it to me. His office wasn't far from my home, so I told him I'd drop by.

I saw Rob Langford getting out of his truck, and he was wearing jeans, boots, and a rattlesnake belt. I asked, "What do you do for a living?"

He said, "I sell land."

I told him I was about to graduate from FSU, and it turns out Rob was in the same fraternity, a KA. He said, "You know, I could use a Florida guy on my team."

Rob was the broker for a company that was based in Bainbridge, Georgia, and they sold large tracts of recreational (hunting, fishing, lifestyle) and agricultural properties in the tristate area. I asked what I had to do to get in the business, and he said get a Florida real-estate license. We decided to meet the next day to talk further, and he gave me a light grilling. He just wanted to see where I was at. Rob explained that I wasn't going to get paid (it was strictly commission), and that I had to go to real-estate school and pass a test to get a license—basically pay for the privilege.

After that meeting, something came back to me. I had once found myself sitting next to the president of the World Bank, and I'd asked his advice on a career. He said, "Do what you love, and the money will come." That always stuck with me. So many people are miserable in their careers, and I didn't want that to be me. Life's way too short. I had a small retirement from the Army, so I could get by. I wasn't married and didn't have kids to support. So, I signed up to take the real-estate course the following week and finished it. I was already scheduled to go overseas for a Wounded Warrior Soldier Ride, so I studied for the state test on both legs of the flight. When I returned, I took the test and passed.

Once I was licensed, Rob lived up to his side and made me part of his team. He referred one property to me that they'd had listed for two years. I had some rapport with the seller—his son had just returned from Afghanistan—and within a few weeks, I had my first sale. I started getting referrals and listings and ended up having a really good rookie year.

Two years later, when Rob decided to launch his own company, he asked if I wanted to become a partner. It meant I was going to have to leave all my listings, but I could tell Rob was a winner—we weren't going to starve. We weren't afraid of hard work, and so we launched Southern Land Realty in the fall of 2013.

As you can imagine, I set my goals very high for my first year. We finished ahead of projections. Rob turns to me occasionally and says, "Are you still glad we did this?" The answer is always yes. I've grown a lot. It really was a sink-or-swim deal. And that's the best part. You can't just measure your success by monetary results—quantitative—it's really that plus relationships and how much you've learned. As long as you're not stressed out of your mind. I had the first-year jitters, and we had some setbacks, but we learned. The good still outweighs the bad. I like to tell people I've defended the land and worked the land; it's now time to help other people discover its bounty.

Rob and I rent office space from one of the best land minds in the area. Everitt Drew wears round rimless glasses, and has a nearly bald head and a huge smile. He's considered the godfather of land sales in what we call the Red Hills region. Everitt has taken me under his wing and often gives me and Rob free advice. When I sit back and look at all the extras I get in this job, it's unbelievable. I've been on the other side; I came from nothing. I know I can learn from the best if I choose to listen.

ACKNOWLEDGMENTS

Many people deserve credit for not only making this book possible but also putting up with my coauthor and me during its development. I'd like to start with recognizing the team at Inkshares for their initial interest, which helped us feel like there was something special to this story. Larry Levitsky was instantly on board and eager to help, which allowed us to go forward in confidence, firing on all eight cylinders. It's been a good partnership.

My fiancéee, Stephanie, was patient and supportive, putting up with me locked away for hours in concentrated effort during story development. She did things to make it easier and was understanding when dinner had to be delayed, even after she'd worked a twelve-hour shift at the hospital ICU.

Much of this manuscript was written the year that I started a new real-estate venture. The first year is hard for any start-up, and I'm grateful to my business partner, Rob Langford, who not only understood when I wasn't available for meetings, but encouraged me and even became one of our financial backers.

For all the guys I served with and learned from, who had an impact on me—thank you. For those who helped save me after the blast—the soldiers who got me out of there, the medics who put me back together, and the medical personnel who kept me positive at Baghdad ER, Landstuhl Medical, and Walter Reed—I wouldn't be here without you. To those physicians who are named in this book, and those who are not named, I'm forever grateful. To all the nonprofit organizations that have helped me and continue to help other wounded service members, you are unsung heroes. You give us hope.

Our initial draft editor, Diana Hume George, was a constant source of affirmation and wisdom in the process. She coached this narrative out of a fifty-three-year-old writer and thirty-three-year-old soldier with grace and style. And our development editor, Tegan Tigani, kindly provided the polish, as she said, "To make the story shine even brighter."

Julie's husband, Jim Bettinger, took the backseat on this wild ride, putting up with his wife's extreme emotions, from giant sobs to shrieks of laughter as she stitched the story together. Thank you, Jim, for loaning her to this special mission.

ABOUT THE AUTHORS

Army Staff Sergeant Luke Murphy (Ret.) served two tours of duty with the 187th Infantry Regiment, a component of the 101st Airborne Division. He was medically retired in 2007 after being catastrophically wounded in an IED blast. Post-injury, he graduated from college, competed in marathons, and helped disabled veterans enjoy hunting and fishing. Luke is a motivational speaker and a partner in Southern Land Realty, specializing in rural and recreational land sales. Find him at LukeMurphy101.com.

Julie Strauss Bettinger is the author of a collection of essays and coauthor of four books. She was editor of *Tallahassee* and *Emerald Coast* city magazines as well as the *Sheriff's Star* and *All Points Bulletin*. Julie holds a Master of Fine Arts in Creative Nonfiction from Goucher College in Baltimore and a bachelors and masters degree from Florida State University. Find her at JulieBettinger.com.

PHOTO CREDITS

GRAND PATRONS

Blasted by Adversity: the Making of a Wounded Warrior was made possible in part by the following people who backed the book on *Inkshares*.com. Thank you for believing in this story.

Babette Smith

Trapper Freeman

Brian T. Buss

Cynthia R. Geeker

David D. Cureton

Emily and Tim Lockard

Gary C. Goodman

Heidi King

Initus, inc

James A. Bulger

James F. Kennedy

J. Everitt Drew

Jim Bettinger

John Laurence

John Nguyen

John S. Schrader

Joseph A. Kelley

Kathryn A. Stich

Ken Cashin

Kyle Poulson

Lauren Meek

Leslie N. Rupp

Leslie S. Redding

Lindsay & Dylan Murphy

Lonnie Maier

Mary Doug Wilgus

Matthew B. Martin

Matthew Hindra

Matthew Sellick

Matthew Spinks

Maura M. Yanosick

Maxwell D. Ramsey

Michael G. Atlee

Misty Dawn Pollock

Richard Stuart II

Robert D. Staton

Robert E. Arbogast

Robert R. Tope

Robertson Langford

Sandy Plante

Seth Palmer

Shelley S. Jerige

Steven Shalloway, B co 3/187

Steven M. Diniaco

Thomas Patterson

Timothy J. Baltes

Todd & Jeri Hunter

Warren Hamilton Smith

William G. Smith III

INKSHARES

9 781947 848818